RECYCLING MADRID

ÁBALOS & HERREROS

ACTAR
A

VILLAGE HALL AND SQUARE
COLMENAREJO, MADRID 1997-1999

The initial intention of paving a small square in a village within the Metropolitan Area of Madrid caused us to propose that the only available site be occupied with a village hall that was meant to strengthen civic life. For the square, we proposed an outline that was capable of reorganizing the unorthodox group of elements that were to be preserved, while the hall was thought of as both a covered extension of the square and like a tensed enclosure of its incomplete body. To materialize both ideas, an extremely light and permeable constructive system was used, finished with natural or recycled materials that allow continuous changes of image and very different uses of the space. The project changes the hierarchies and the perception of the space, setting up a dialogue between memory and the present with the intention of reflecting the changing condition of these peripheral areas.

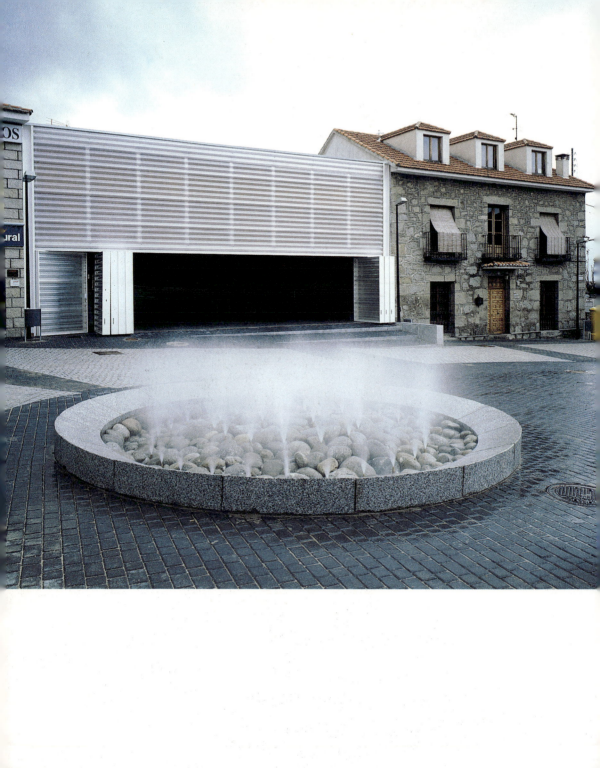

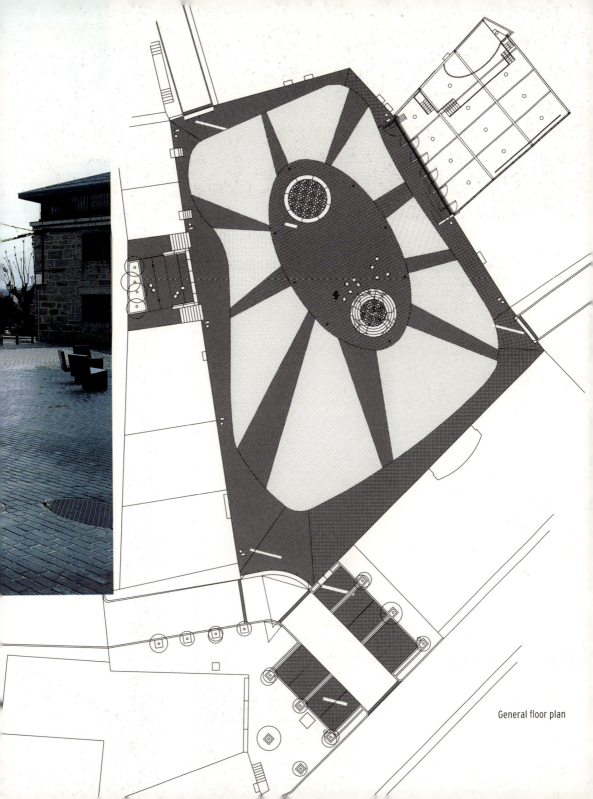

General floor plan

RECYCLING MADRID

IÑAKI ABALOS & JUAN HERREROS

Twenty years ago we studied Madrid as a solid artefact, isolated in the landscape and walled-in by its infrastructures. The city was described as an almond in the middle of the Castillian Plateau, surrounded by its ring road, the M-30. The renowned writer and engineer Juan Benet drew the city as a 38km long ellipse, whose axes measured 9 and 5.5km fig. 1. That Madrid which, for better or worse, became a modern city, had an elemental zoning plan that laid out its most noble residential suburbs as well as the service zones to the north-west and the industrial areas and the commuter suburbs to the south. Further afield, there was nothing.

1

Today this description has become outdated and obsolete, not only because the city has exploded due to new infrastructures and a different political and metropolitan organization, but also because social behaviour has changed. The way in which the city is used and perceived has changed forever. We cannot continue to think of it with that figure-ground contrast model that we knew as artificial action versus nature. Today, Madrid is a metropolitan conglomerate of 8,000km² shaped like a large triangle, surrounded by the "Castillian Sea" and the fields of La Mancha: it is a true island. This triangle has a size and a topographic configuration that is similar to those of Mallorca, with its mountainous cornice to the south-west (the Guadarrama mountain range) that protects, at its feet, a sloping platform that is traversed by the rivers that discharge into the Tajo figs. 2-3-4. An island in which the lives of five million inhabitants are organized (12% of the Spanish population) trying to find relationships with a physical medium of great contrasts and that passes from the exuberance of the North to the extraordinarily hard plateaus of the South. This city-island is a fragile and artificial ecosystem that has large untouched areas as well as others that are extremely dense in which, little by little, it is becoming more evident that the preservation and restoration of the former –the old "ground"– has as much importance as the built space –the "figure". Together they make up the indivisible form that, today, we call Madrid.

But it would be naïve to think of it as a conventional island. It is more akin to the centre of a gigantic atoll, with its corona –the Spanish Coast– hyper-populated and in permanent vital and dialectic tension with its centre [fig. 5]. This image allows us to imagine that we are living in a singular place with an exciting geographical location, and not on the plateau-like almond that we inherited. From this point of view, Madrid is

2-3 Madrid with its parks highlighted   4 Topographical diagram of Madrid   5 Spain-atoll. Diagram

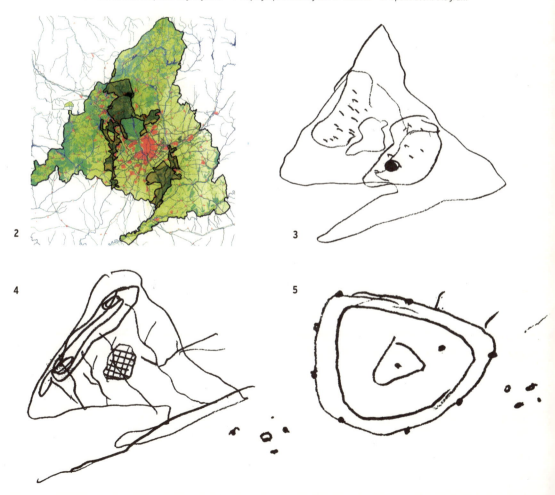

an evolving city of five million inhabitants —the third largest in Europe after London and Paris— that is begging to be recycled with imagination and pragmatism, adapting it to a culture whose sensibilities and way of being have dramatically changed. Working in this city has become, despite the evidence that constantly disputes this statement, an exciting exercise. Like all islands, Madrid is a micro-cosmos, the model of a possible world —or of all possible worlds— made up of materials that form a special conglomeration, always unusual and paradoxical. We recently described it as an amalgam, a material that was unknown, until now: a conglomeration of natural, artificial and immaterial elements (fluxes) that are simultaneously porous and fibrous, with dense and stable areas, loaded with memories, and vast diluted expanses that are devoid of character and are almost liquid, made up of antithetical elements that have broken with the precision of the traditional limits between the natural and the artificial. And we added: if we were Modern architects we would think of this city in moral terms and this would make space for reformative policies. But it seems more necessary and, if you wish, more linked to the practice of architecture, to find a poetic substratum in this magma and to understand it as something that invites us to test a new gaze, through which to reach a critical dimension. This material, the dissolution of the natural-artificial opposition, at all scales, leads to a work programme that is none other than to rewrite the stance of contemporary man in the face of the world [1].

The first work that we developed was the construction of three residual water treatment plants along River Guadarrama, in the north-west of Madrid. We began by thinking of the opportunities that building with the techniques and the scale of large infrastructures would offer, but soon realised that it was far more interesting to work as gardeners, creating didactic landscapes, resolving the boundaries with the land and allowing that the purification process and its optimization create their own logic, setting up an accord between the natural and the artificial [fig. 6]. The buildings prop themselves up on the land and keep technical and visual control from these positions [fig. 7]. In this way we learned to establish a body to body relationship with the physical medium and also that each

Water treatment plant in Majadahonda. 1986

project contained the whole city in fragments. It was enough to have an idea, a way of looking that would make this miracle possible.

We have now completed a project that is symmetrical to the one that we have just mentioned. If the former was located in the fluvial valleys of the North, this one is situated on the south-eastern corner of Madrid, on the lowest part of its orography, on a chalky terrain onto which the city has historically discharged its sewage, as well as all sorts of residues. This is a place whose name, Vacíamadrid [2], provoked Ortega to reflect. The project was to build the plant where all of Madrid's domestic refuse was to be recycled: 2,800 tonnes per day, one million tonnes per year. As the dump was centralized at this unique point, we found ourselves dealing with the largest recycling plant in Europe. Once again we have tried to design an organisation that is inspired by an accord between the starkly naked landscape and the technical processes. Because the separation of recyclable products takes place through gravitational processes, the plant is placed upon a hill to reproduce this mechanism, accommodating the whole beneath a roof of vegetation and wrapping the whole with recycled polycarbonate. In this way the architecture reproduces both the place and the technical processes that make it possible. We proposed –and this decision gave us, partly, the necessary advantage with which to win the competition– to endow this project with public and political content, making visible something that had always been hidden. To achieve this we decided to group together an countless number of small pieces, buildings, workshops, offices etc., within a single volume in such a way as to obtain a large construction that is capable, because of its size, of setting up a dialogue with the whole of the surrounding landscape and its topographical accidents. Therefore we composed a constructive system that explored what was possible today, from an environmental point of view, with market techniques. We wanted to obtain with these catalogue procedures, not only an illustrative image of this sensibility, but also a monumental effect that is similar to that found in engineering works of a certain scale, such as a clear and diffuse light whose enveloping intensity might unify the various activities.

We also included a programme for visitors to the plant (a route that runs above it beginning in a museum-like space where the relationship between everyday life and recycled products is shown) in a desire to convert an industrial shed into a public building.

Two buildings complete the enclosure: a control point where the lorries are weighed on entering the plant, and a hermetically sealed building for the making of compost. The former, inspired by the metaphysical character of the landscape, is organised like an imposing megalithic "trilithon" raised in the middle of this impressive nothingness.
The second is made up of an extension of cells, full of organic material, and traversed by a large, well-lit control room. It spreads itself like a mastaba on a relatively low level, as it attempts to camouflage itself with the landscape.

The periphery is no longer something that is distant and picturesque with which, perhaps, to aesthetically enrapture oneself, but is, rather, like a true laboratory in which to test universal ideas that are also valid in the corona of the atoll that encircles Madrid, the rest of the world or even in the bourgeois nucleus of the city.
It is precisely in this nucleus that we have had the opportunity to develop a singular project. It is an urban villa for the family of an important public figure: a banker, an art collector and, like the other members of the family, a keen amateur sportsman, especially enjoying swimming and gymnastics. By coincidence, the Villa FG a residence situated on the *Colina de los Chopos*[3] (*El Viso*) was developed parallel to the construction of the recycling plant and occupied the same amount of energy and time. This coincidence allowed us to take curious return journeys, significant exchanges about the nature of the project.

As one can deduce from the name of the area where the villa is situated, it is located on one of the most humid, fertile and green hills in Madrid. It is a plot of land that is adjacent to the mythical *Residencia de Estudiantes* where Lorca, Buñuel and Dalí lived together and faces one of the city's most important private gardens. South-facing, with magnificent views, (both close and distant) the site is located in a fantastic place, but is, however, very small leaving the villa with very little open space around it.

We thought that it should have the artificial features of a large, compact, traditional house, whose composition and the scale of its openings reveal a palatial character. At the same time, given the lack of space on the plot, the volume demanded that it be "planted" so that the volume of the building itself should dissolve into a vertical garden.

To give form to this palatial character we grouped together the different parts of the programme onto four floors or superposed houses -the workshop house, the museum house, the hotel house that holds privacy, and the spa or "beach" house, as we prefer to call it. We composed a route for the art collection with them. Each floor is an autonomous universe with its own formal codes, developed room by room, and is traversed by an ascending promenade that is intentionally complex and intricate, contrasting with the simplicity of the floor plans. In order to "gardenize" the house, we thought of radicalizing the project's materiality. This intention should be interpreted literally rather than metaphorically, so that the entire house, and not only the façade, becomes planted. The plant material, the sun, the water, the trees and the wind could be used from a figurative and also a constructive, programmatic and energy point of view, creating a special technical experience that would take all of its energy from the humid and fertile character of the *Colina de los Chopos*. The various natural materials are organized in a horizontal and vertical system that traverses the house, giving it a unique character as well as a twinkling light that bathes the space in a way that is inverse and complementary to that of the promenade which is laid out for the viewing of the collection. In some way, ideas that are tried out in the most humble corner of the suburban land are allowed to be 'recycled' for a privileged occasion, in the centre of the city and for the upper middle-class of Madrid. A middle-class that, on the other hand, has gone for forty years without being able to build a relevant house...

We have also recently completed a small public project in a village in the north-west of Madrid's corona. We were asked to pave what could hardly be called "a square". The project was a group of extremely incoherent buildings that were grouped around a void that had no other value than to preserve the memory of the origin of this nucleus, Colmenarejo [4].

Our intention has been to try to give shape to the changes that this nucleus, today immersed in metropolitan life, has undergone and also to this ugly and unconnected built mass, through some buildings and a treatment of the paving that attempts to make the existing irregularity coherent. To achieve this we have used possibilities offered to us by ornamental forms, designing a continuous floor with a shape similar to that of a guitar which has been tensed and deformed by the various concerns that we came across. Something that is capable of evoking traditional shapes and the most immediate plastic compositions that

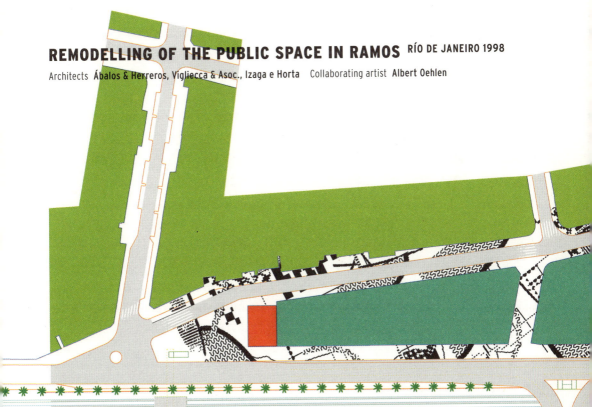

REMODELLING OF THE PUBLIC SPACE IN RAMOS RÍO DE JANEIRO 1998

Architects **Ábalos & Herreros, Vigliecca & Asoc., Izaga e Horta**   Collaborating artist **Albert Oehlen**

relate to our sensibility. However, the intervention also consisted of taking advantage of those public spaces that remained untreated, to close the space and to create enclosures —an open-air canopy and a public hall— with which to activate civic initiative and to make it possible to use the space in new ways. The hall was conceived of as a minimal filter between the exterior and the interior: a weightless roof with a translucent front that, simultaneously, gives a continuity to the urban façade and radically contrasts with it. It is a veil that is supported between the pre-existing structures whose interior finishes are of natural wicker. Its exterior enclosure is a sheet of polycarbonate, the lower part of which unfolds like an accordion, opening and integrating the room into the square, illuminating it at night, like a vertical sky.

For us, it has the value of a miniature manifesto, almost secret, a light reply to the question about whether architecture repeats itself from its beginnings. How is a room without a predetermined function and that expresses our time and stance built? Other later projects, such as the one in Algeciras, the AVE train station in Zaragoza, the Gymnastics Pavilion in El Retiro Park in Madrid or the Ramos project for Rio de Janeiro have come about through some ideas that were outlined here:

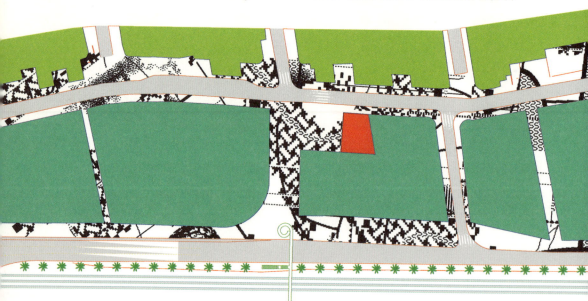

the materials, the ornamental design of the paving, the idea of an abstract room or the reduction of the project to just one characteristic feature.

Through this collection of buildings and projects, we have investigated what could come about by thinking of architecture as still-life: like a collection of natural and artificial elements that form expressive compositions or constructions. The natural-artificial duality has shown us that its character is no longer antagonistic, but that it is an amalgam, like a material of today, full of new possibilities. It is a mixture of nature, memory and technique. With it we not only try to celebrate a certain sensibility. We also try to work with the most precise and difficult question: "And now, what shall we do?"

These images or buildings avoid an organic geometry, just as they avoid minimalist autism. They try to individualize a stance that is distant from a fascination for the geometric complexity of a new avant-garde that

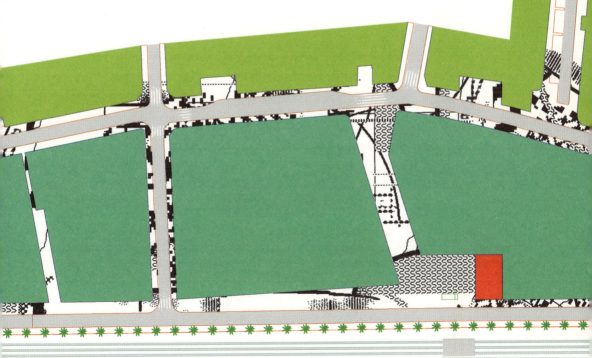

reproduces the pro-science attitude of the Moderns, which is now applied to new paradigms: fluids and chaotic, unstable phenomena. It would be too literal and too nostalgic to continue to try to be at the vanguard by reproducing the attitudes of a century ago. Why repeat this uni-directional fascination for science rather than turning our attention to the material practices in which our everyday life is dissolved? Our work is impregnated with objects, advertisements, films, songs, novels, essays, journeys, videos, lazy holidays, fantasies, exhibitions, fashions, forests and excesses as well as with books on biology, chemistry or fractal geometry. This is the natural-artificial amalgam on which it is nourished.

For this reason, we also feel distant from an ascetic and self-sufficient minimalism. Frankly, we see it, more and more, as being much closer to the art of puritans, of a whole army of right and left-wing dogmatists who only feel at home in a world that is closed and tidy, and who turn their back on anything that might threaten this. We are searching for an architecture that is mixed and hybrid that is also able to vibrate with the moment: light, simple and intense.

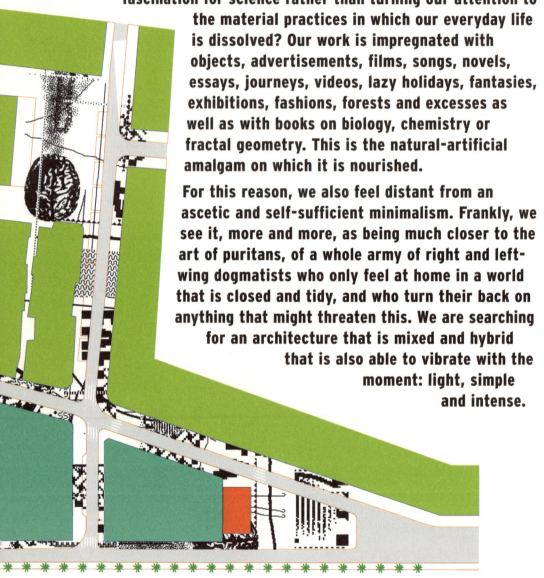

We feel that we are well accompanied on this quest, advancing along unforeseeable paths with others who do not wish to be trapped in this false reductionist dichotomy that obliges one to use fluid geometries or to be minimalist. The question that we ask ourselves is, "How can an architecture that considers this dual approach that is the product of the past be? What is an architecture after the minimal and the celebration of chaos like? Is there life beyond this? Do we, who are indifferent to this perverse cage, have anything to say?"

This text began by talking about recycling the image of Madrid that is like an isolated almond in the desert. However, recycling this idea seems to require a wider and, perhaps a more attractive recycling. It is the very idea of the architect who requests a jolt that can, perhaps, only come from a revised idea, not only of the city, but also of the attitudes, methods and inherited conclusions. **ÁBALOS & HERREROS**

1 See "End of the century still lifes", *El Croquis*, issue 90, pages. 4-23, 1999.
2 *Vacíamadrid* literally means "Emptymadrid". (Translator note)
3 *Colina de los Chopos* literally means "Poplar Hill". (Translator note)
4 *Colmenar* is the Spanish word meaning a group of beehives. (Translator note)

VILLA FG

This is an urban villa for a middle-class family in which an art collection was to be exhibited and an area for gymnastics and swimming were to be built. As one can imagine from the name of the place, it is one of the most humid and fertile areas of central Madrid, facing a wonderful garden with magnificent views and orientation. We proposed a compact construction that would have openings and a scale that would give it a palatial character. At the same time, given the small size of the plot, the idea was to dematerialize this volume by turning it into a vertical garden in such a way that the plants, the sun, the water, the trees and the wind should take not only a figurative role, but also one that deals with constructive, programmatic and energy issues.

Inside, the different parts of the programme are organized into four storeys or stacked houses −the workshop house of work, the museum house of representation, the hotel house of privacy, and the bath house or "beach" dedicated to physical culture. These houses are traversed by an intricate and ascending *promenade* along which the art collection is exhibited. Contrasting with it and in the opposite direction, a humid and twinkling light bathes the house giving it a special character.

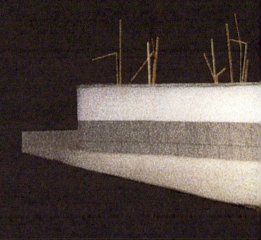

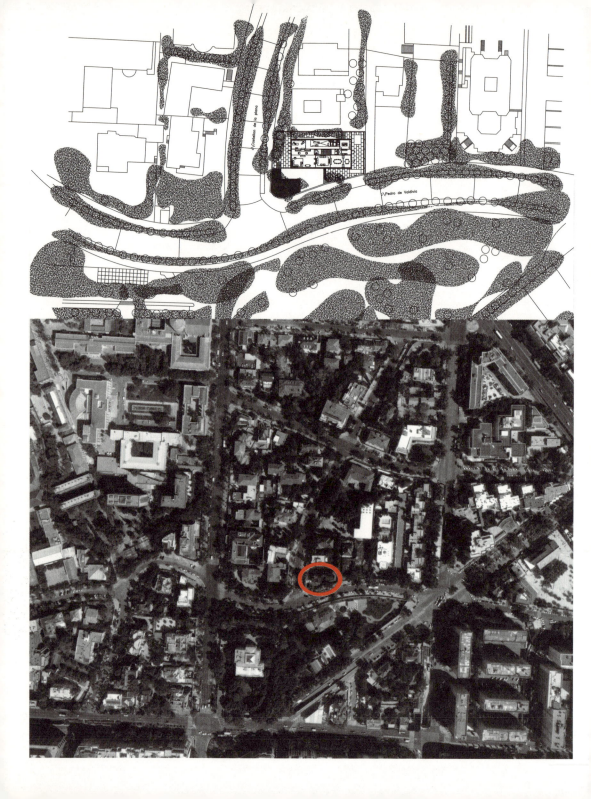

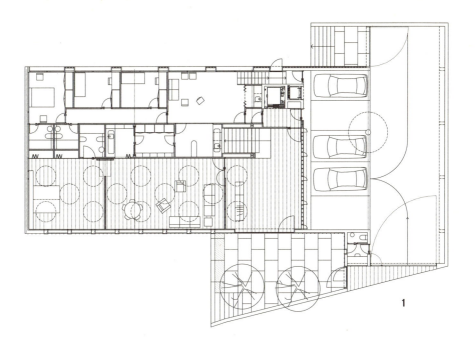

1

2

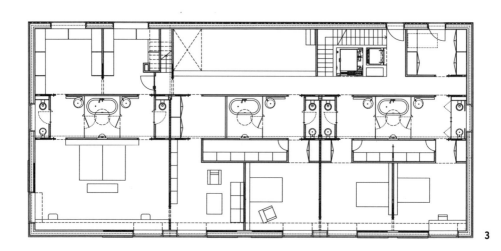

3

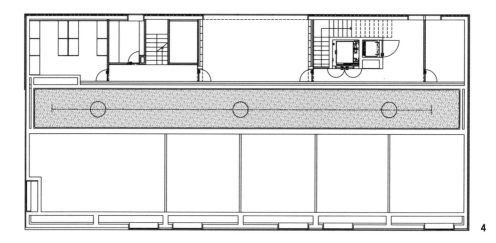

4

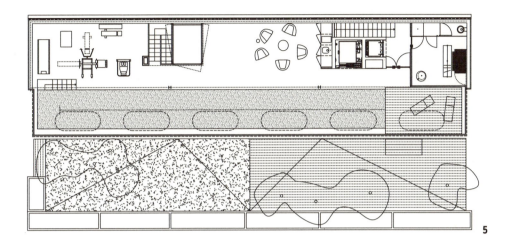

5

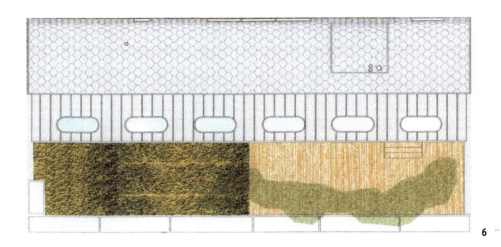

6

1 Semi-basement floor plan   2 Ground floor plan   3 First floor plan   4 Second floor plan   5 Third floor plan   6 Roof floor plan

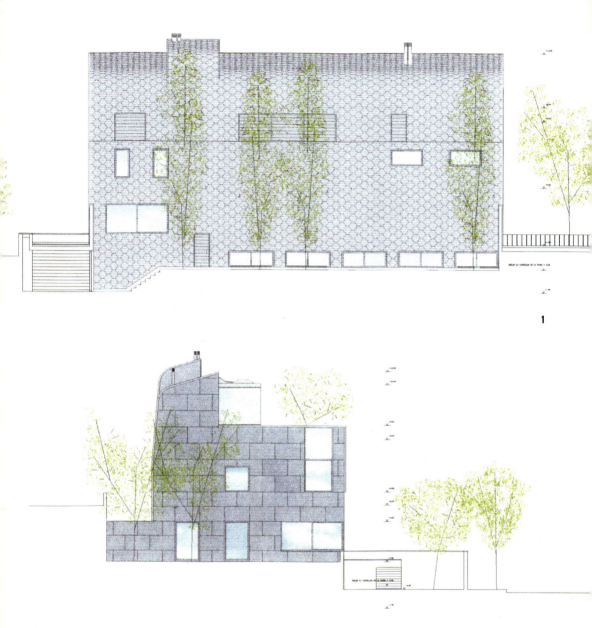

1

2

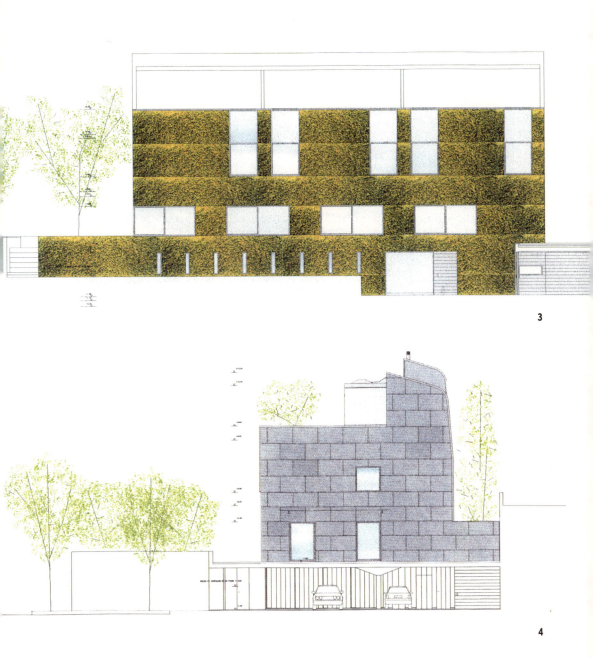

3

4

1 North elevation   2 West elevation   3 South elevation   4 East elevation

Transverse section

1 Roof and north elevation
Exposed white concrete (H-200) wall/slab
4 cm, 35 Kg/m³ projected polyurethane insulation
Discontinuous wood sleepers and wood plank flooring
Rubber waterproofing (roof and sloped wall)
Ventilated air space
40x40 cm Adeka zinc scales

2 Pool enclosure
Balcony Carbe Glass retractable glazing system
8 mm tempered glass

3 Skylight
Aluyjoma fixed glazing with thermal break

4 Roof
Concrete (H-200) slab
3 cm polystyrene insulation
2 mm Zinco GmbH self-healing rubber membrane
Roof gardens:
-LB80 root protection membrane
-Cement topping slab
-Polystyrene sheet
-Floradrain Fd60 filled with gravel
-Teak draining deck
-Organic soil layer
-Grass + trees
-Perimeter of rounded white marble gravel
Perimeter of roof:
-3 cm extruded polystyrene

-Sleepers
-15x80x3 cm bolondo plank flooring with stainless fasteners and open joints
-Stair with bolondo treads on an aluminum structure
Paved areas:
-Cement topping slab
-Self-adjusting telescoping pedestals
-Aluminum structure
-15x250x3 cm bolondo plank flooring with stainless fasteners and open joints
-Oil for ultraviolet protection

5 Guardrail
Single piece, solid teak handrail
Low wall of Knauf double plasterboard

6 Bedrooms
Partitions and ceilings of Knauf double plasterboard with recess for shutters
Motorized concealed shutters of double 12 mm enameled MDF panels
Enameled calibrated steel plate baseboard
Teak plank flooring with rigid joints over cement
Floor treatment with oils for ultraviolet protection
Rehau warm/cool radiant floor over expanded polystyrene
Concrete (H-200) slab

7 Corridor
Partitions and ceilings of Knauf

double plasterboard with central recess for lighting and acoustic insulation in partitions
Enameled calibrated steel plate baseboard
Teak plank flooring with rigid joints over cement
Floor treatment with oils for ultraviolet protection
Rehau warm/cool radiant floor over expanded polystyrene
Concrete (H-200) slab

8 Stair
Solid, one-piece, teak treads

9 Main stair
Partitions and ceiling of 16 mm marine plywood finished with natural maple veneer
Stair treads of solid 15x30 cm slaty quartzite stone

10 Living rooms
Partitions and ceilings of Knauf double plasterboard with perimeter recess in ceiling and acoustic insulation in partitions
Enameled calibrated steel plate baseboard
Teak plank flooring with rigid joints over cement
Rehau warm/cool radiant floor over expanded polystyrene
Concrete (H-200) slab

11 Service area
Exposed, white concrete (H-200) ceiling
Partitions of Knauf double plaster-

board with acoustic insulation
Enameled calibrated steel plate baseboard
Polished colored concrete floor with quartz and marble aggregate
Rehau warm/cool radiant floor over expanded polystyrene
Concrete topping slab
Pre-stressed floor slab
Air space

12 Multi-purpose room
Exposed, white H-200 ceiling
Enameled wood panel partitions as shown in detail drawings
Enameled calibrated steel plate baseboard
Continuous paving of polished colored concrete with quartz and marble aggregate divided with aluminum joints into 20 m² sections
Rehau radiant floor warm/cool over expanded polystyrene
Concrete topping slab
Pre-stressed floor slab
Air space

13 Facade base on south elevation
Double Knauf plasterboard
Air space with guides for sliding shutters at bedrooms and sliding windows in the other openings
Concrete (H-200) wall
Plant facade composed of waterproofing, porous polyester fiber panel, stainless steel 4x4 cm Techline mesh with slopes every 2 meters

Hydroponic plants as shown in detail forming 2x5 meter plant blocks with the identical plant motif
Aluyjoma exterior double hung bedroom windows with climalit securit 12+6+8 insulated security glass
Aluyjoma windows with climalit 5+6+6 insulating glass
Exterior aluminum sills, lintels and jambs
Interior sills, lintels and jambs of calibrated steel plate with baked enamel finish

14 Facade base on east and west elevations
Double Knauf plasterboard with IBR 60 fiberglass batts
Thermal insulation
Air space with guides for sliding windows at the openings
Exposed white concrete (H-200) wall
3 cm lead gray slaty quartzite stone cladding with stainless steel anchors, joint pattern as shown in drawing

15 Site wall
30x150x5 cm solid stone coping of slaty quartzite
Concrete (H-200)
Cement plaster
Rasallt stucco
Protection
Interior and exterior slaty stone base 150x15x3 cm

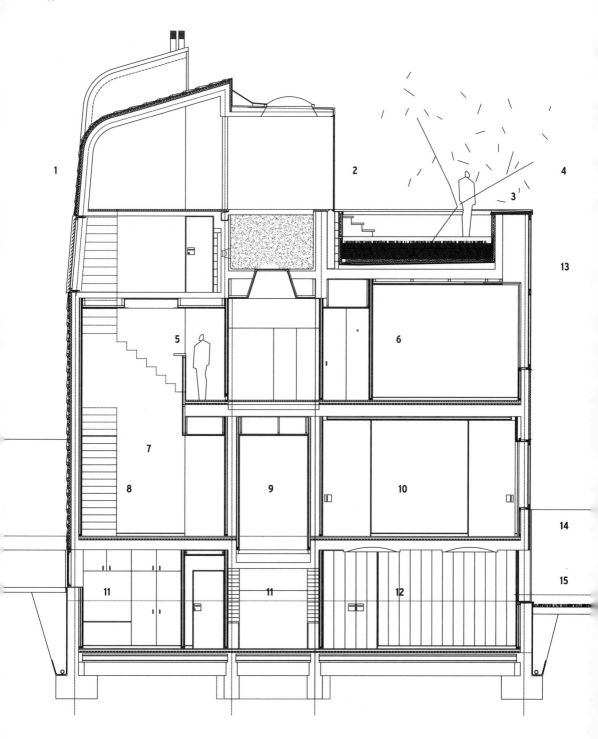

Interiors 1 Multi-purpose room   2 Entrance hall   3 Main bedroom   4 Living room   5 Bathroom and toilet

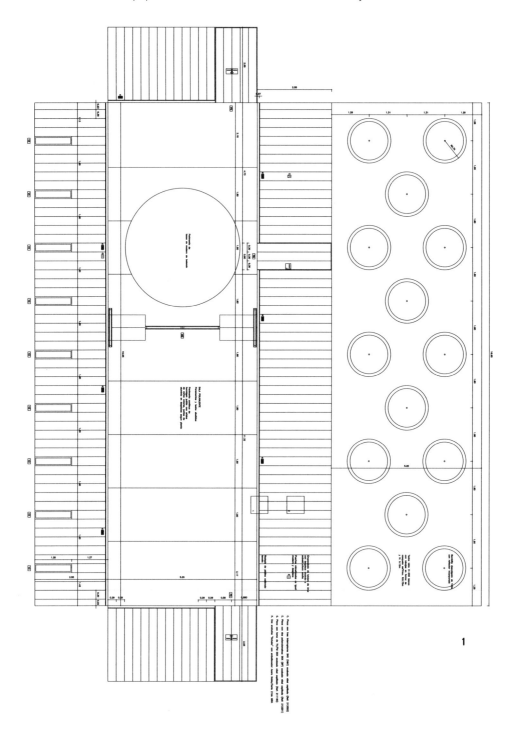

1

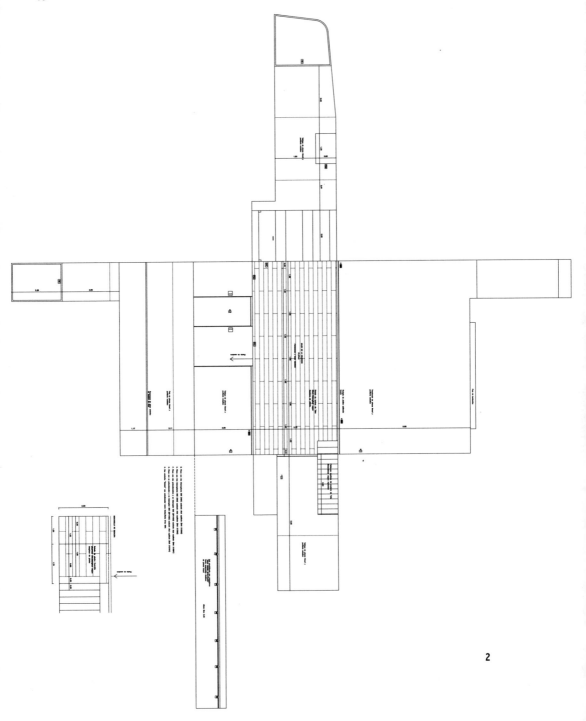

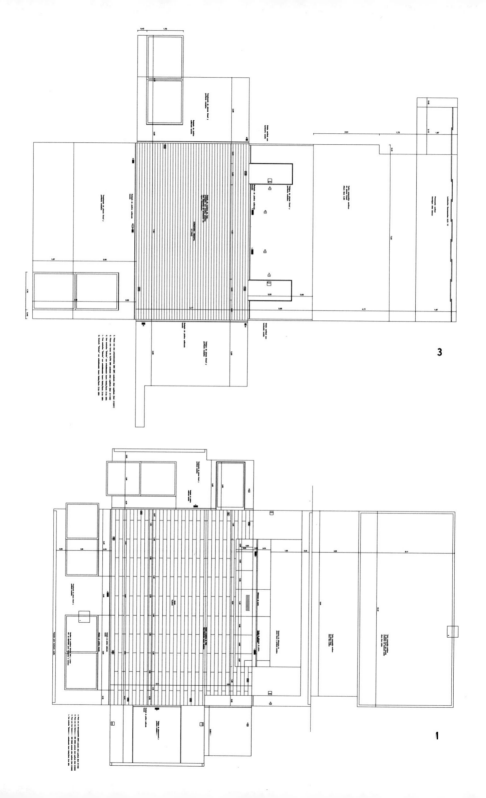

3

1

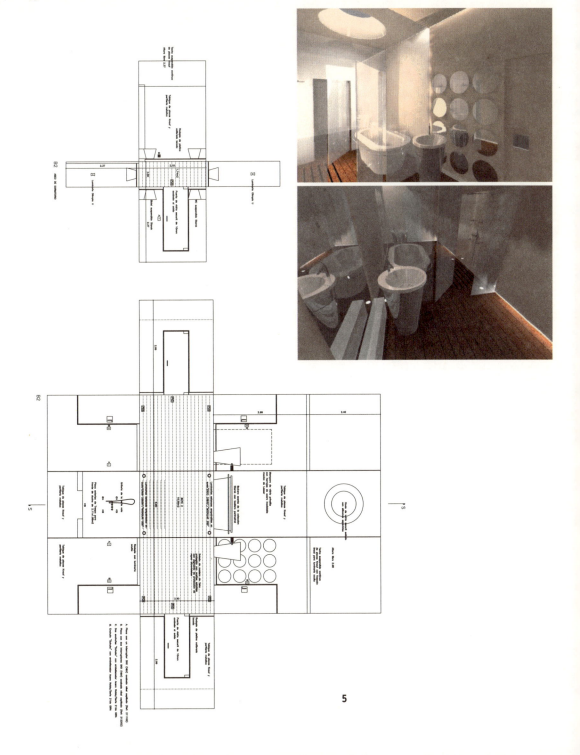

North facade. Detail **Amado Ramos**

Vegetable wall **Patrick Blanck**

EL MIRADOR: MIXED-USE TOWER

The project attempts to express, with an architectural gesture, the beauty of the geography of Algeciras: the bay, The Rock and the Straits of Gibraltar, the proximity of Ceuta and Africa, the cork forests that surround the city... For this we propose a construction that, from one single body, splits into two towers from one great public viewing platform. This body opens strategic holes in the most notable topographical accidents, establishing a physical relationship with them, while the section is organized as a building-up of privacy which increases with height.

The programme feeds itself from this relationship with the physical medium: a museum of the Bay of Algeciras and the Straits of Gibraltar make the base of a publicly managed industrial hotel that is meant to promote new industries and businesses that are linked to the the port's activity. At the top there is a sports club that is dedicated to physical culture. A group of residential or professional lofts crown the whole.

A mixed façade is envisaged, with strips of glass alternating with others that are made of recycled cellular polycarbonate, which protects ventilated wall cavities or end translucent areas. When it forms a cavity wall, this element protects a sheet of natural cork that serves as insulation in such a way that the whole acquires an ambiguous and evanescent presence, transparent and translucent —with the associated nocturnal effects— but also natural and artificial, tectonic and immaterial, a conglomeration whose image wants to represent the sensibility of contemporary society towards the city and the land.

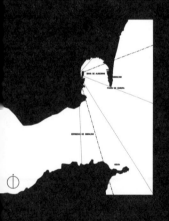

1

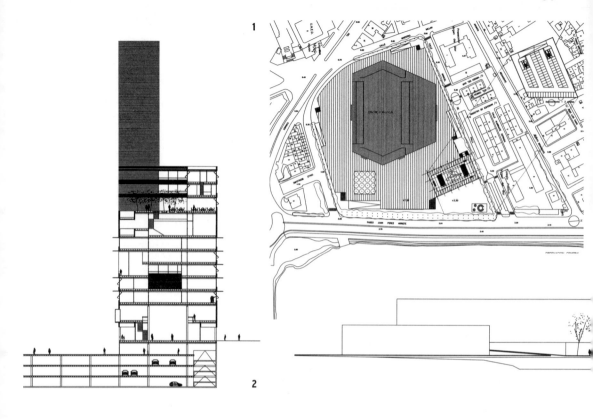

2

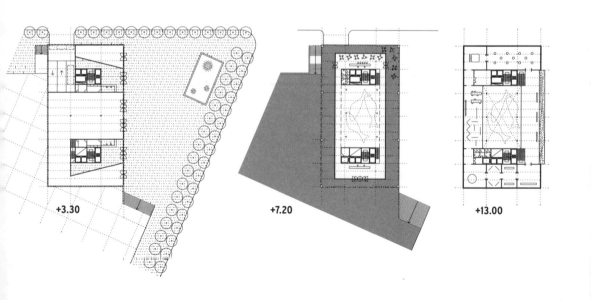

+3.30

+7.20

+13.00

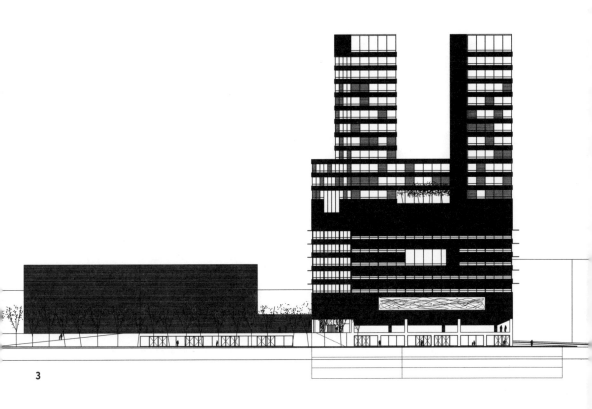

3

1 Site   2 Cross section   3 Main elevation   4 Plans

4

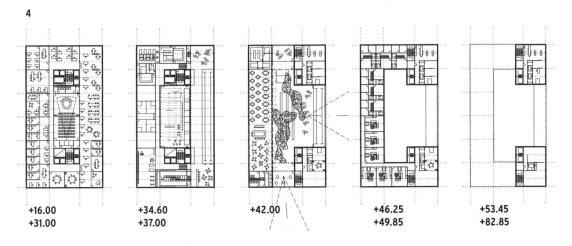

+16.00
+31.00

+34.60
+37.00

+42.00

+46.25
+49.85

+53.45
+82.85

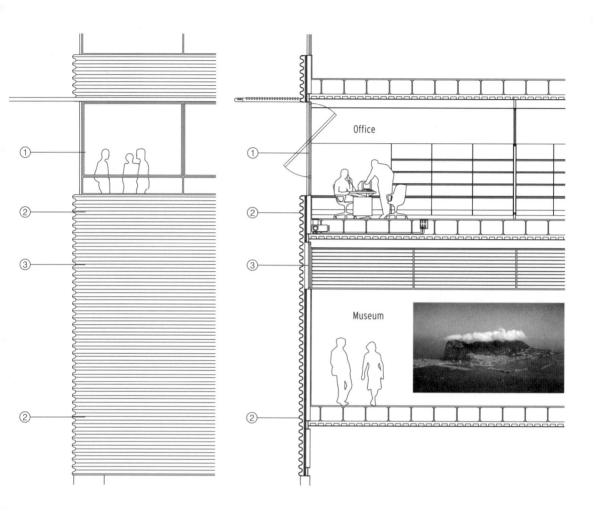

Facade detail   Claddings: 1 Transparent. Glass   2 Opaque. Cork + Polycarbonate   3 Translucent. Glass + Polycarbonate

Section   Program -3/-1 Car park   0 Commercial use   1/2 Museum of the Bay of Algeciras and the Straits of Gibraltar
3/7 Industrial Hotel   8 Sports and Health Institute   9 Terrace Club Restaurant   10/20 Housing and lofts

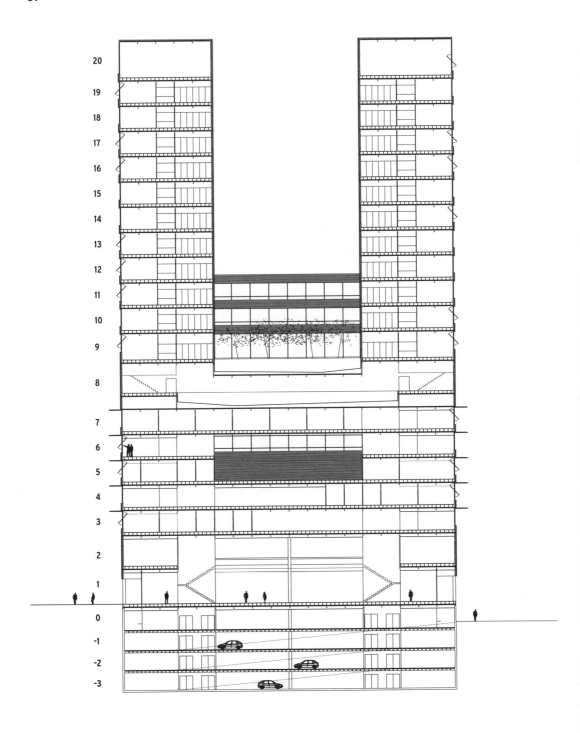

IGNASI DE SOLA-MORALES

In his never-delivered American Lectures, Italo Calvino proposed that the idea of lightness be one of the six themes that should be thought of as most important for the new millennium. Iñaki Ábalos and Juan Herreros, whose work was included in the *Light Construction* exhibition at the MoMA in New York in 1995, were selected as representatives of a certain type of lightness on proposing their architecture. Lightness [1] is understood here not only as a physical condition that is obviously used metaphorically, but also as a certain moral attitude towards those decisive actions that are represented by architecture.

On the one hand, perplexity. We are concerned with a lightness that is the result of a non-dogmatic stance. Their architectures do not postulate, they do not even make categorical affirmations. They propose, they probe, they even play without, at any moment, trying to unfold universal principles, lines of action for the future or any sort of salvation. Today, perplexity seems to be an honest way of positioning oneself before things that are so complex and changing and so accompanied by noisy advertising.

Their built architecture and their projects are attractive because they propose, with a certain amount of modesty, a different path for resolving what are, in many cases, problems that have always existed. Their architecture is neither revolutionary nor is it even radical, if this last word is understood as an objection to the totality: as something that comes from the origin. There are neither totalities nor origins, nor are there any roots so evident that they can be paradigms of the action of architecture. Sometimes they make discoveries, they reconsider established subjects, they use technologies, materials, gestures and forms that, for various reasons, are stored in the archives of those ideas that nobody has known how to use in an ingenious and creative way.

Their relationship with technological innovation is ambiguously innovative. For many people, the possibilities that are offered by technological advancements provoke a feeling of both attraction and fear. Submerged in a world where nuclear energy, genetics and pan-information are perceived as enriching possibilities that are, at the same time, full of risk and horror, an architecture that does not flee from technological advancements and the possibilities that come with them, and that also displays its caution, its ironic, sometimes-biased approximation, that searches for ways around the overwhelming and oppressive messages that the *high-tech* world almost always proposes is particularly attractive.

Technology without technological rhetoric, the incorporation of ingenuities and rationalizing methods that never become immutable rules are, not only, the practical means of their way of working, but are a transcription from the technological side of the moral lightness with which their architectures are presented to us.

We must not mistake this aesthetic and ethical content for any kind of symbolic use of architecture. The material form of the buildings of Ábalos & Herreros is neither the support nor the vehicle for idealistic messages. One of the most outstanding features of their work is the decisive importance taken by the material starting points in each project.

This is surely the clearest link that their work has with the best architecture of the Modern Movement and what always gives a freshness to those things that are born with their feet placed firmly on the material possibilities.

We have seen architecture of steel and of concrete, of glass and of titanium. For some, this is an appropriate way of classifying modern production and of explaining the close relationship that exists between technique and architecture. The work of Ábalos & Herreros is far from this tellurian and Faustian idea in which the conjuring of the natural forces serves to illuminate the work of architecture.

Their work seems to be, on the contrary, of *bricolage*. This French word is to be understood with all of the significance that the anthropologist, Levi-Strauss, gave to it when he explained the many techniques used by certain primitive tribes to make important objects.

To uninhibitedly use available material repertoires, to find resources from industrial production that have yet to be exploited in the construction of buildings, to experiment with the possibilities of pieces, rubbers, plastics, car technologies, agriculture, packaging or distribution in order to solve, in some other way, those problems that are inherent in architecture. This is one of the most stimulating and creative aspects of their material starting point.

What is attractive resides, above all, in the ingenious ability to use a product that was created for some other purpose in the building process. Without doubt, it is about some sort of *estrangement* whose main ability is not produced at the level of meanings but at that of signs. All metaphors bring a semiotic *estrangement* like that proposed by the linguists of the Prague School.

What is new in the architecture of Ábalos and Herreros is that this displacement is produced at the first level of meaning, which is the one given by the choice of the material and its technology.

The architecture that we call Modern has often searched for, in the boat, the automobile or the space craft, icons with which to load its designs with meaning. What is less frequent is that this meaning is not produced at this prearranged level, but at previous levels that are directly linked to the virtualities of the discovered materials: true Duchampian *objets trouvés* that are formed at the starting point of a meaning of a totally different nature.

To this innovative technological bricolage, we must add another, no-less-refined, meaning. It is the fundamental sense of recycling that dominates the material basis of their work.

It is not at all strange that a work that is as strong and as ambitious as the collection of proposals for Madrid's municipal rubbish dump in Valdemingómez becomes a paradigm of all their work. The new rubbish dump, the buildings for the treatment of residues, the interpretation of the landscape and its role in the growth of a large city make this experience a conceptual nucleus with a very special significance. It is clear that this work, done with speed, pragmatic sense, bricolage, smart material but also with the ambitious overview of the whole, is a landmark in their production. This is not the moment to give an exhaustive description of the building or of all of the work that is still underway.

However, there are enough indicators for us to be able to understand the way that Ábalos & Herreros approach the contemporary problems of architecture. The fact that they have grasped, with great talent, a process, an urban system, an industrial activity that is halfway between the interests of the public and the private and, above all, a theme for the recycling of residues that in itself constitutes a completely innovative challenge which Edward W. Soja would call post-metropolitan architecture.

Architecture always appears when a clear agenda that defines intentions and procedures already exists. What constitutes architecture's contribution to situations like these is not so much the contribution of completely different methods, but its ability to understand them in relation to the site, the landscape, the city.

The new Madrid Rubbish Dump is, all of it, a recycling operation, not only because the processes that occur within it transform refuse into usable products, but also because the ideas of the complete organic cycle and continuity are the main concerns of the proposal.

The contemporaneity of this discovery does not lie only in the fact that it has given shape to a typical problem of today that before was dealt with in a totally passive and intransitive manner. Through the appropriation of a way of seeing the city's material processes in their nomadic wanderings across the land and its permanent transformation, the architecture and the landscape that narrate them become an echo of the internal organicity with which these processes are presented to us.

The fact that the discussion about recycling deeply nourishes the Valde-mingómez project also means that in other projects the incorporation of processes, of organic activity, of gardening or *ars-topiaria* (as the authors themselves like to call it with a historicist twist of humour) is also a new front for reflection and proposing that has only just begun.

Gilles Deleuze and Felix Guattari, especially in *Mille Plateaux*, develop politics for contemporary energies: that is to say, a way of describing the land, events, history and conflict as a multiple process that is in a permanent state of expansion and contraction. Ábalos & Herreros' way of thinking seems to respond profoundly to this way of perceiving, interpreting and dealing with reality.

Because of this, beyond their discrete lightness, their anti-dogmatism and their transversal use of the technology of which they have become intelligent spokesmen, the greatest contribution of their work to the contemporary sensibility and reflection is their ability to synchronize with a thought and a feeling that has their roots, their *rhizome* perhaps, in the difficult conditions of today's societies and cities.

Ecological architecture? Please! No! The temptation to label the last works of Ábalos & Herreros with a term that is as ideologically loaded as *ecological* or *ecology* is like dropping a heavy slab of indifference onto their work.

It is precisely an interest and a way of operating that transcends these sorts of disciplines and ideologies. What opens up before us, on the threshold of the new century, cannot be a new crusade in favour of Mother Nature and her sustainability, but an enormous repertoire of questions, possibilities, of treatments related to live processes to which certain architectures have been able to contribute with their own discourses.

In an attempt to understand more about how this architecture is made, I would like to propose three formal notions that I see to be repeatedly present in their work and that somehow clarify all that I have said so far.

From the point of view of form, the work of Ábalos & Herreros seems to take an attitude of a certain indifference. It is as though the outline or the scale of their buildings and their treatment of the surfaces were not of any great importance, but rather, an almost casual outcome of some unimportant decision.

This seems even more apparent when, on going over their works, we realize that there are no fixations about certain stereotypes. Their buildings seem to be made up from established repertoires of well-known building types about which they have, by the way, made theoretical studies of great scope.

It takes place as though the starting point is the tower block, the pavilion with a free-plan, the block of flats or the box for tertiary use that is

CONSULTATION FOR THE POBLE NOU DISTRICT BARCELONA 1999

Architects **Iñaki Ábalos, Juan Herreros** in collaboration with **Renata Sentkiewicz**

1 Lofts. Uses include professional office, showroom,
   consulting services, residential and/or hotel use
2 Longitudinal section. The space opens onto a park at
   ground level and to an artificial mountain

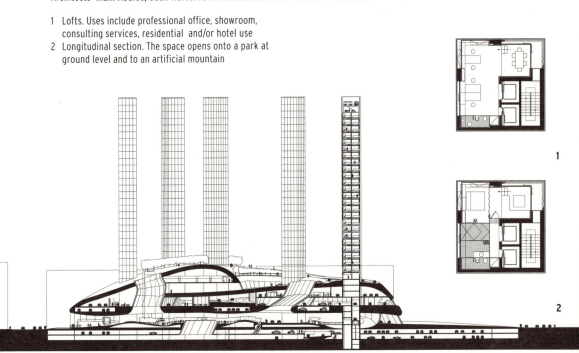

1

2

divided into units that are used as examples of known or even commercial architectures. From this point they always produce a twist, a distortion, a gesture that is delicate yet firm and that modifies conventional approaches. It is a way of doing that is, somehow, optimistic. They are individual, special and circumstantial rather than new programmatic proposals.

The architectures of Ábalos & Herreros are not experimentalist in the sense of proposing new forms or different building types, nor do they search for paths of innovation in new geometries, fractals, undulations or folds. A sober and disillusioned relationship with what there is, with what is available on the market, leads them from what is conventionally accepted, economically buildable and technically viable from practical points of view. But if this is the starting point, of course, the development of the project does not end here. Slight distortions, gestures, hybridizations and, above all, an exquisite attention to the surface are the processes that make their work singular.

Because of their synthetical character, we find clear indications of this sensibility in some of their competition projects. The dispersion of the towers in the project for the Cerdà urban block in Barcelona involves a multiplication game in the style of Daniel Buren, at the same time that the reduction of the solitary house evokes the impossible projects of John Hejduk. The two, almost Loosian, laconic towers of the Algeciras project distort the theme of the phallic landmark of the lone tower, converting it into a doubtful, centre-less, duality. As an idea, the Bonn project transforms the conventional service building into a surprising hill or urban cowpat: an informal metaphor for the dissolving of the usual prepotence of public buildings into the landscape. The extremely elegant project for the AVE train station in Zaragoza, from the typology of the great hangar that is served by two vestibules that face it, to the way that the balconies hang over the tracks, is resolved through the ethereal gesture that responds to the design of the roof. Like the gusts of air of Oriental painting that Juan Navarro Baldeweg evokes when he explains the forming of a shape, this outline that is closer to abstract expressionism than to a purely technical decision makes the building fly. This is something that, on the other hand, is very adequate because it

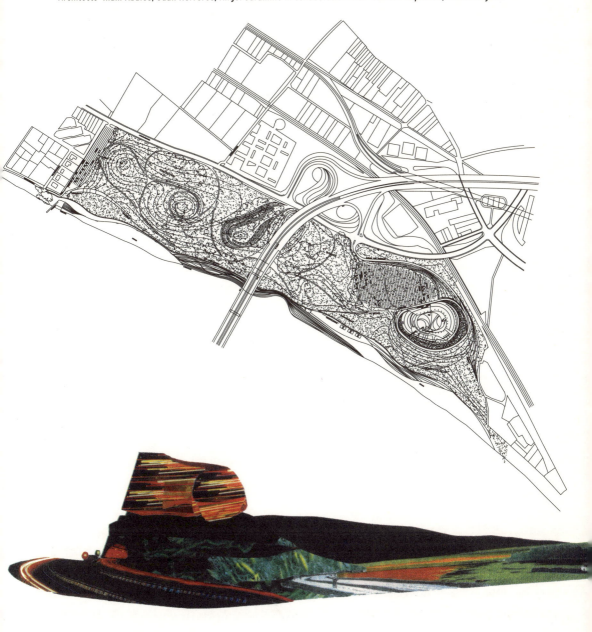

suffers from a scale that is somewhat uncontrolled and from an obvious lack of references in the city.

All of these gestures are personal insertions, individual expressions if you wish, that are carried out on the much-too-inert mass of the established types. It is interesting to observe, however, that they add to an architecture that is always somewhat distant and cold, manipulations that have no other origin than the personal gesture, the sensibility of the moment and a certain justification of subjective contamination in the face of so much conventionalism and anonymity.

But where this open crack seems to be particularly prolific seems to be in the exercise of defining the surfaces.

An underground link seems to connect the Baroque sensibility: "I am only my appearance," as Gracián said, with that of Surrealism: "Words, begin in the mouth," according to the phrase of Tristan Tzara. They have a certain way of happening in reality. Not only is ornament no longer a crime today, but also the tattoo, graffiti, and body piercing seem to be the most powerful forms of inscription of today's culture. It is, therefore, not at all strange that the architecture of Ábalos & Herreros is particularly sensitive to these levels of work and signing.

What is surprising and attractive about the projects of the Green House or the Villa FG, of Colmenarejo or the Rubbish Dump is the contrast between the organizational and spatial decision that is relatively hard and, at times, conclusive. It is almost always alien to excessive details in the form, the multiplication of the openings or the entrance of light and the extreme attention that is given to the surfaces: to its texture, its colour, its vibration, its feel.

In contrast to what has been, for years, the neo-vernacular and the remains of the neo-liberty architectures with their obsessive attention to detail, material boundaries, changes in direction and the so-called design, the architecture of Ábalos & Herreros seems to assume a certain extensive monotony of its planes that are stretched in walls and pavings, and altered in roofs and facades. On the other hand, the inventive discovery that is often the fruit of the recycling of what we spoke of

AVE TRAIN STATION AND INTERCHANGE TERMINAL

ZARAGOZA 1999

The project is thought of as the most direct and efficient manifestation of the fluxes of the people who use the station in relation to the movement of the trains. A large, symmetrically curved roof allows us to follow, at all times, the movement of the people. This generates, in a very unitary way, the sequence of necessary spaces: the connection with the urban transport systems, the double vestibule –arrival and departure– with their services and waiting areas, the conveyor belts that lead to the platforms and the parking of vehicles on the roof, so that the spaces that are perceived by the user are, thus, unified by a single gesture that organizes and shelters the main character, the train.

This simple scheme houses the Service Centre on the upper face of the roof –offices, hotels and other facilities– which foresees the programme transforming what, from below, is a monumental roof into a large curved square that gives access to these facilities and allows one to see the landscape and the town of Zaragoza from an exceptional vantage point.

This offers a true public space that will integrate this large intervention into the collection of buildings and public spaces that are representative of the city's identity.

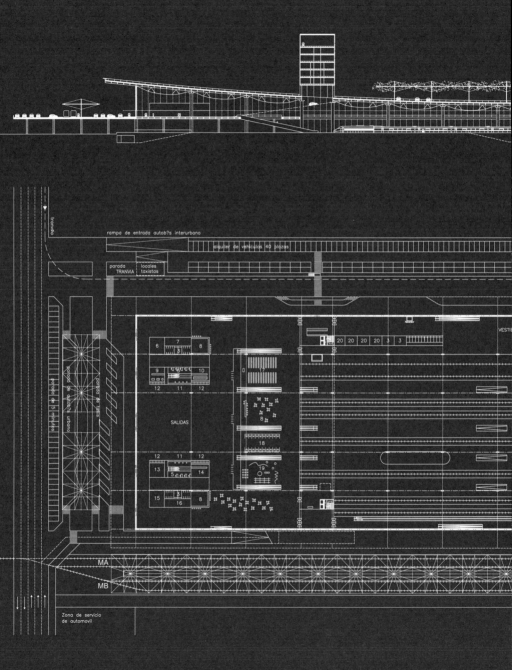

rampa de entrada autob?s interurbano

alquiler de vehículos 40 plazas

parada TRANVIA | locales taxistas

tranvía

parada de autobús urbano

parada de 5 minutos

parada de taxis

6 | 7 | 8
9 | 10
12 | 11 | 12

17

SALIDAS

8

18

12 | 11 | 12
13 | 14
5

19

15 | 16 | 8

20 | 20 | 20 | 20 | 3 | 3

VESTI

MA

MB

Zona de servicio
de automovil

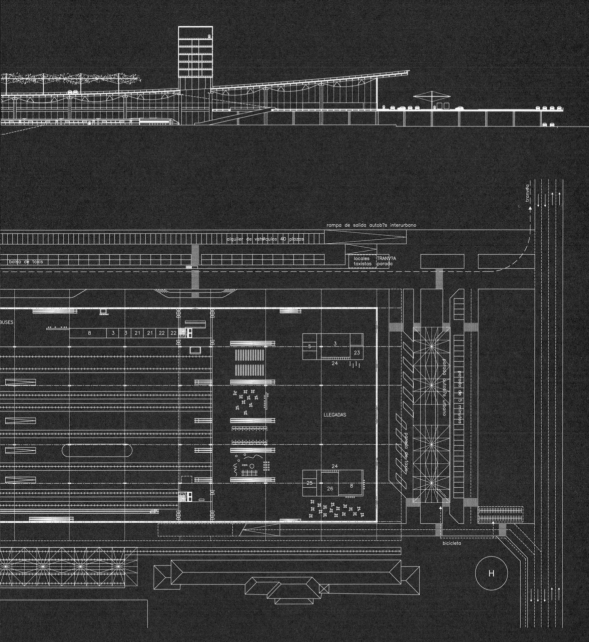

rampa de salida autob?s interurbano

alquiler de vehículos 40 plazas

bolsa de taxis

locales taxistas

TRANV?A parada

BUSES

8   3   21 21 22 22

6   3   23
24

LLEGADAS

24
25   26   8

bicicleta

tranvía

parada de taxis urbano

parada de 5 minutos

H

HALL PLAN

Train departure hall: 1 Waiting room. 2 GIF office. 3 Toilets. 4 VIP lounge. 5 Offices. 6 Pharmacy. 7 Police. 8 Cafe. 9 Photography shop. 10. Bookstore. 11 Ticket windows. 12 Ticket machines. 13 Medical assistance. 14 Computer store. 15 Gift shop. 16 Baggage check. 17 TV room. 18 Computer stations. 19 Daycare center.

Bus hall: 3 Toilets. 8 Cafe. 11 Ticket windows. 20 Control stations. 21 First Aid. 22 Guard station.

Train arrival hall: 3 Toilets. 5 Offices. 8 Cafe. 23 Tourist + Hotel information. 24 Automatic tellers (Bank/Parking). 25 Car rental offices. 26 Kitchen.

earlier and that, in any case, is aware of the potential of the material, the matter to be built can, in its unstoppable process of innovation, offer, as a contribution to surprises, the disequilibrium of the foreseen and the taste for the new as part of the architectonic text.

Concentrating creative efforts and bringing about a space for personal discovery in surfaces also means an agreement with the fragility of what they propose and the almost playful character of these inscriptions. It also means a certain decrease or, at least, a terseness of the most important expressive adventures.

The adjective, "superficial", normally has no other use than give a reductive value to a proposition. "Superficial" seems to mean the opposite of "profound", "essential", "radical", and it becomes too close to "banal", "useless", "futile" or "insignificant".

Perhaps one of the most interesting paths of contemporary culture has to do with the opposite discourse. As Lyotard has pointed out, all information and all communication are consumed on the surface. The body in its skin, the object in its wrapping, the city on its interface, the network on the screen. Underestimating the surface as the place where our contacts and interchanges occur is the result of a transendentalism that aims to reach what is deep and essential by avoiding a journey on the surface, its ability to transmit and its synaesthetic effects.
An architecture that takes surfaces into account can, as Riegl points out about late-Roman art, be an architecture that is somewhat disenchanted, that has cancelled essentialist discourses and hopes for great messages of unity and humanistic synthesis. Sliding across the surface is the acceptation of the limited duration of the effects and the unavoidable necessity of the fact that we widen our understanding through them.

The lightness of the recent work of Ábalos & Herreros, their oblique interest in technology, their sensibility for organic continuity and recycling as an inventive attitude find the clearest and the best evidence of their indisputable contemporaneity in their investigation about the surface. IGNASI DE SOLÀ-MORALES

1 The author stresses the difference between *levedad* and *ligereza* that does not correspond exactly to the difference between levity and lightness. Here, the word lightness has been used for both. (Translator note)

GREEN HOUSE

POZUELO, MADRID 1997

The project is located in a typical area of the middle-class suburb, in which low-density housing, voids, public facilities and small masses of pine trees intermingle giving shape to an idea of an urban life that is in contact with nature. We decided to be extremely direct and to stress this desire through the use of gardening techniques. Thus the whole house can be understood as an example of a giant *ars-topiaria*. This is an idea that is not alien to the fact that it will be a home for a landscape architect. The sloping topography is taken advantage of to build a house that has a continuity with the natural land, avoiding the differentiation between the house and the garden: the whole house is garden and the whole garden is house. The project is a topological mechanism for the arranging and modelling of the land to increase and to gain the maximum enjoyment from those weak stimuli of the landscape: the pine trees, the near-by stream, the setting of the sun over the skyline of Madrid from the house's highest point... Natural views and artificial views: green machine.

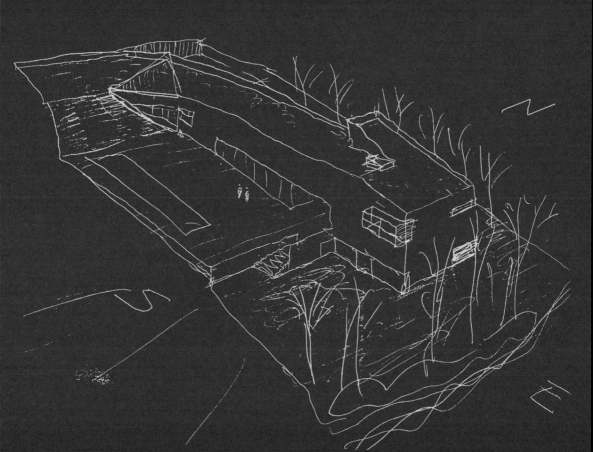

PEP XURRET

Dear Iñaki Ábalos and Juan Herreros,

I belong to the generation of not-so-Young Catalan Architects who grew up with the enthusiasm of a city that was optimistic about its urban transformations. A city that trusted architects and encouraged us to participate in the reconstruction of its identity... and so we did. Together we were known as the "Generation of the 80's" (I was in the poster), and together (but each in his own office) we won hundreds of small competitions and prizes. We built tens of Olympic Projects and, little by little, we took permanent teaching places in the Barcelona School of Architecture (which at that time was the world's second-best school). Meanwhile, Madrid seemed to stimulate itself from different perspectives. The city encouraged other artistic sectors, leaving young architects with few possibilities to exercise their shared enthusiasm. The projects that we knew of seemed to be subject to the ineffective dynamics of politicians and the stagnant academic heritage. Madrid-City was no longer the place to re-launch the collective... Madrid's young architects, like you, had to wait and to prepare intellectual strategies for defining new professional and territorial limits in order to reconstruct Madrid-Country, where you could begin to work again. While we learned through rebuilding, you learned through thinking about how and where to do so.

I write to you from Madrid on my way to El Retiro Park in search of the newly-built Gymnastics Pavilion. It's been a long time since I have visited a new building in the centre of Madrid. Lately, all of the interesting works, including yours, have been built on the outskirts which, for you, has been the area of impunity where you could freely develop your metropolitan theories.

Now, as I enter the El Retiro Park, I ask myself if these theories can be applied to the city's historical centre with the same optimism. I am afraid that your project, although it is built in the centre, was thought of for the periphery. (This is exactly the opposite to what we did in Barcelona, where the projects for the periphery were thought of as a continuation of the built city).

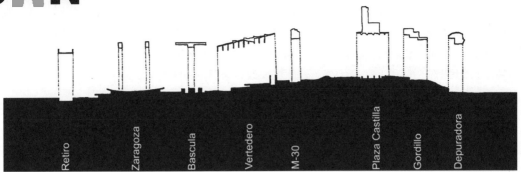

Retiro · Zaragoza · Bascula · Vertedero · M-30 · Plaza Castilla · Gordillo · Depuradora

1

I approach your building. I recognize it because it tries to disappear, this is its stance and its presence. From far away, it looks like a plant structure that reminds me of an enormous fence integrated into the park, even though it is made monumental by its size as it absorbs its immediate surroundings for its own benefit, appropriating the site's identity. Its attire is not one of camouflage but it dresses for the unique occasion of the reorientation of the site.

It is a Pavilion, an isolated building that stands with a certain arrogance upon a place which it attempts to domesticate (normally the periphery). It stands like a piece of furniture that orientates itself, uses and anchors itself to the site without anchoring itself to the landscape. A light piece of furniture whose lightness and nomadic ability could allow it to disappear to stroll amongst other commissions... (I would say that I saw this pavilion on the outskirts of Simancas dressed as Colmenarejo in Spring). Were the building to leave, only the anchors and the topographical mechanisms would remain. They are, in the end, its physical compromise with the place fig. 1.

Anchors assume various forms in your projects: they are sometimes built plinths (Ayuntamiento de Cobeña, RENFE), hollow plinths (Plaza de Castilla, Colmenarejo, Zaragoza), illuminated plinths (the Ministry) or topographical plinths (water treatment plant, Gordillo, rubbish dump). The buildings settle, they support, they gather together, they rise and they levitate, almost identical, above an artificial ground that is almost always specific.

The preparation of the site allows you to convert all of your projects into astute variations on the pavilion theme. Thus, on isolating themselves they allow the sigfnificance to be isolated, loading its surfaces with new requirements. New resources are repeated in them. They explore possibilities, building them as you build your photomontages: selected, trimmed, scaled and pasted onto the landscape. You load the surfaces with representational and technological hopes, but it is in the anchors where the gesture, the stance and the most tectonic dialogue with the site is prepared.

At last I enter the Pavilion, crossing the section over its symmetrical horizontal plane that reflects the two gymnasiums: interior and exterior, above and below respectively. One is excavated four metres into the land, building the footprint that announces the building. The other is raised three metres above the park, assuming the star role in the scene.

I leave the pavilion and I look again now that I have learned the section. It is a pavilion like the others, although it is raised only because the land is lowered, giving scale to the surroundings. The radicality of what is present, of the visible, counterbalances the care with which the land is prepared.
I climb onto the roof with no hope of seeing the horizon. Once there, enclosed within the green climbing plants and Madrid's electric sky, I realize that the shortest route is not the straight line. I realize that cities need peripherical gazes like yours and, by the way..., to hell with Olympic inertia.

Yours, PEP XURRET

This is a letter that was sent on the occasion of the exhibition *Recycling Madrid: Ábalos & Herreros* that was organized by the Vocalia de Cultura de Barcelona of the COAC (Culture Department of the COAC).

GYMNASTICS PAVILION IN EL RETIRO

MADRID 1999

It is a three-metre-high platform, surrounded by trees and enclosed by translucent walls to accommodate an excavated volume in which offices, changing rooms and storerooms were placed on two storeys leaving a double-height gymnasium lit from above. The proposed system of metal grilles will allow for both the protection of the services and for vegetation to grow around it, thus wrapping the whole. This organization allows the roof to be used either as an open-air gymnasium or as a tennis court.

The image that is sought after is one that is close to that of certain plant constructions that are very traditional in gardening, particularly in Buen Retiro where historically have been constructed magnificent examples of spaces built with hedges. By emulating these references the project attempts to create an abstract composition with the plant matter cut away at the edges in such a way that the new construction should seem to be like an amalgam of natural and artificial elements, a plastic composition that will give a characteristic identity to this part of the park.

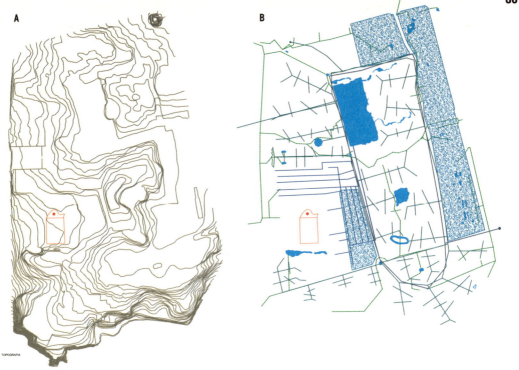

A

TOPOGRAFIA

B

Diagrams   A Siting   B Water   C Trees, density   D Humidity level according to species

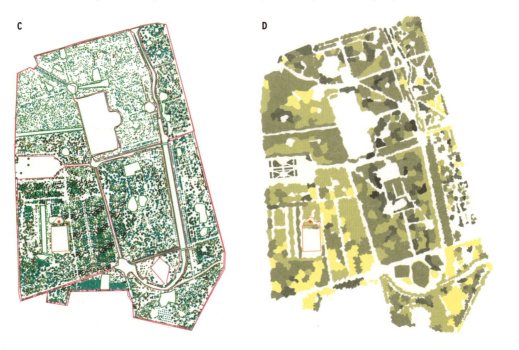

C

D

Plans   1 Offices and park   2 Gymnasium

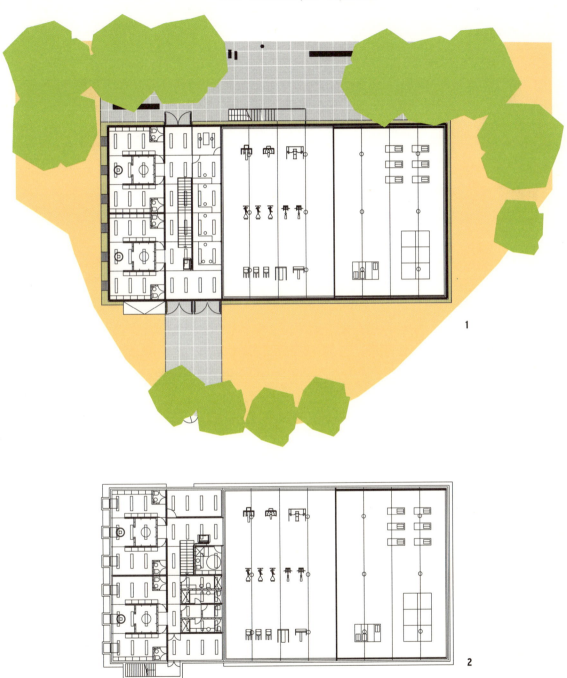

1

2

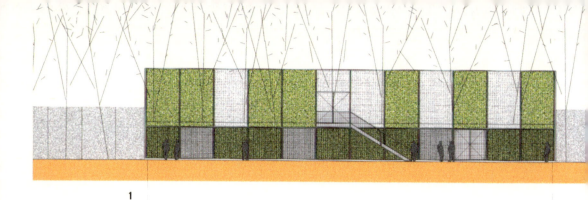

1

Elevations   1 South   2 East   3 West   4 North

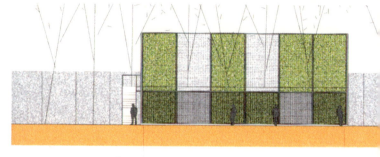

2

**Transverse section.
Interior end elevations**

A Stair
Steel structure
40x100 mm Tramex stainless
steel treads formed by 40x3 mm
strips
Metal mesh guardrail and
perimeter fence

B Perimeter fence
GKD stainless steel metal fabric,
model Futura M. painted in RAL
green to be determined,
anchored and tensed to round
stainless steel bars
on a framework of steel plates,
with baked enamel finish,
forming 500x300 mm and
275x300 cm panels

**C Perimeter gardens
(ground floor - roof)**
Low perimeter brick wall
Separation sheet of synthetic
felt geotextile, 300 g/m² and

perforation resistance of 2.800 N
1.2 mm Intemper PVC waterproofing membrane reinforced with
impregnated fiberglass felt
Gravel drainage bed
Separation sheet of synthetic
felt geotextile, 150 g/m²
Soil with compost mixed with
river sand for planting vines
Planting with Ampélosis + Madre
Selva every 40-50 cm, two
meters high in areas with green
panels above and below
Drip irrigation

D Roof
Lightweight concrete forming a
sloped dome in four sections
without defined edges
300 g geotextile sheet
5 cm Roofmate
1.2 mm Intemper PVC waterproof
membrane reinforced with
fiberglass
300 g geotextile protection
sheet
ø12-18 mm drainage layer of

gravel for leveling and filling the
drainage trenches
Tennisquick porous colored
draining concrete (sand color)
with a minimum depth of 9 cm
Perimeter and anchors of sports
equipment finished in Chapolan

E Ground floor elevation
Perimeter fence
Metal structure
Lexan Thermoclear clip-40
cellular polycarbonate on
calibrated steel plate frames

**F Half basement walls
(gymnasium)**
Exposed concrete 1 face
(interior) with 300x126 cm
plywood panels and rods as
shown on plans

G Basement wall
30 cm reinforced concrete wall
Delta drain waterproofing with
asphalt impregnated polyester
layer

Porous wall with drainage tube
at lower edge, filled with gravel

H Structure
Metal structure 'granallada' of
HEB columns and IPE profiles
18 m solid web girders built up
of welded plates
Finished with 1200 micros white
intumescent paint, Stofire of
Euroquímica, over zinc rust
protection
Mixed slab structure of QL-60 1
mm ribbed decking, with white
baked enamel finish and 12 cm
of concrete

**I Semi-basement floor
(gymnasium)**
DIN double sleeper system (for
sports uses):
Junckers solid beech plank
flooring, press dried, 22 mm
thick and 129 mm wide
Plastic anti-rock membrane on
the reverse side of the planks
Upper pine sleeper, 35x70 mm

every 33.64 cm
24 mm DIN piece (with a
maximum on center distance of
40 cm)
Lower pine sleeper, 45x45 mm
every 41.11 cm
Leveling blocks
0.15 mm plastic anti-humidity
membrane
Perforated maple baseboard

20 cm slab poured continuously
with the foundation over 15 cm
of gravel and insulating sheet
In the gymnasium the upper
surface of the slab is roughened
mechanically floated.

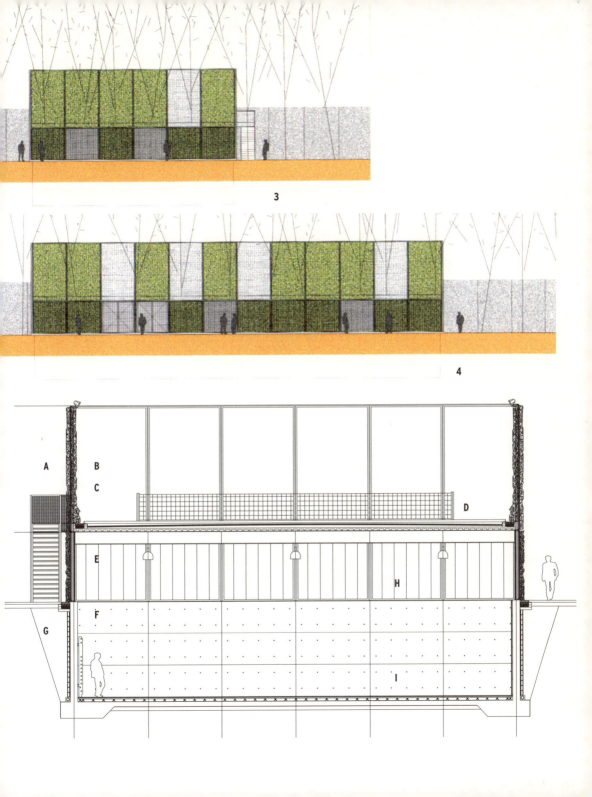

3

4

A

B

C

D

E

F

G

H

I

VALDEMINGÓMEZ DUMP
THE LANDSCAPE TRANSFORMATION
OF MADRID'S OLD RUBBISH DUMP

MADRID 1997

The Valdemingómez area is at the lowest point of the southeastern corner of the district of Madrid. It is a dry and run down land that has, historically, been the dumping ground for the city's waste.

The site is dominated by an enormous artificial plateau that has been built with the refuse that has been dumped there during the last thirty years, while another, of a similar size and with a content of 10% non-recyclable refuse, will grow during the next twenty-five years. Both platforms make up the gateway of one of Madrid Regional Government's great metropolitan projects: the Southeast Regional Park, fed by the waters of the Jarama and the Manzanares. A piece of nature reserve towards which the city irreversibly grows. For this we think that the decontamination of the old rubbish dump —a process that will take at least fifteen years— could bring the economic resources that are needed for generating a specialized piece of the regional park, a "gate", in which to develop a positive gaze towards the extremely hard and beautiful landscape of the chalky lands of the South, just as Alberto Sánchez and other artists did years ago.

A park that is understood as an "area of impunity" where space could be made for those unusual, extravagant and even disturbing uses that, like the rubbish, are expelled from those consolidated parts of the city but which, without doubt, still form part of the urban character of the land. From the biological point of view, such an aggressive public-owned site allows the intervention to be understood as an opportunity to investigate and cultivate resistant species with which to urbanize the residential growth southwards: a municipal nursery that was planted as a machine to reforest the new Madrid. With twice the area of El Retiro Park in Madrid and a similar size to Central Park by Frederick Law Olmsted, we are studying techniques with which to manipulate in a positive way, a landscape, that until very recently has been ignored. We work with smells, with the wind, with the wealth of bird-life, with large-scale earthworks, with erosion, with the speed of various sports, with the characteristic void of La Mancha, with shades of sand and earth, with the distribution systems of biogas...

Diagram of uses

Diagram of smells

Diagram of circulation

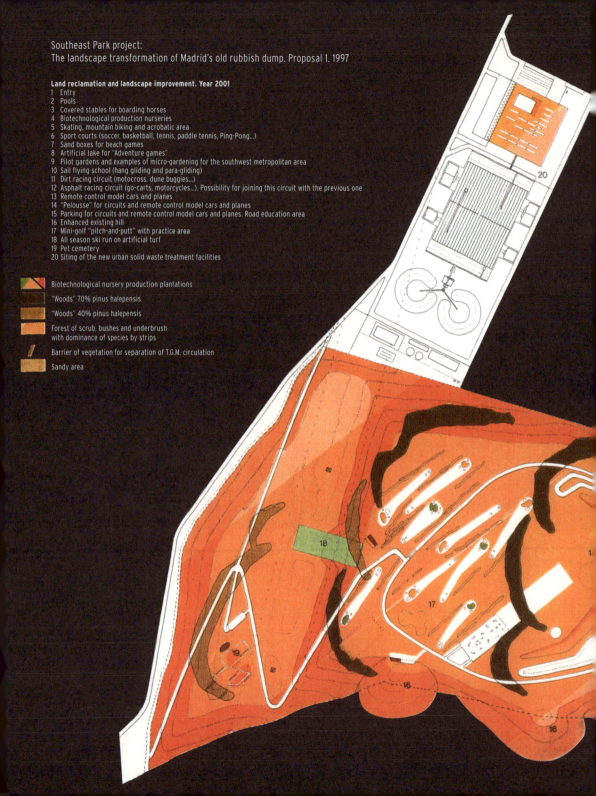

Southeast Park project:
The landscape transformation of Madrid's old rubbish dump. Proposal 1. 1997

Land reclamation and landscape improvement. Year 2001
1 Entry
2 Pools
3 Covered stables for boarding horses
4 Biotechnological production nurseries
5 Skating, mountain biking and acrobatic area
6 Sport courts (soccer, basketball, tennis, paddle tennis, Ping-Pong...)
7 Sand boxes for beach games
8 Artificial lake for "Adventure games"
9 Pilot gardens and examples of micro-gardening for the southwest metropolitan area
10 Sail flying school (hang gliding and para-gliding)
11 Dirt racing circuit (motocross, dune buggies...)
12 Asphalt racing circuit (go-carts, motorcycles...). Possibility for joining this circuit with the previous one
13 Remote control model cars and planes
14 "Pelousse" for circuits and remote control model cars and planes
15 Parking for circuits and remote control model cars and planes. Road education area
16 Enhanced existing hill
17 Mini-golf "pitch-and-putt" with practice area
18 All season ski run on artificial turf
19 Pet cemetery
20 Siting of the new urban solid waste treatment facilities

Biotechnological nursery production plantations

"Woods" 70% pinus halepensis

"Woods" 40% pinus halepensis

Forest of scrub, bushes and underbrush
with dominance of species by strips

Barrier of vegetation for separation of T.G.M. circulation

Sandy area

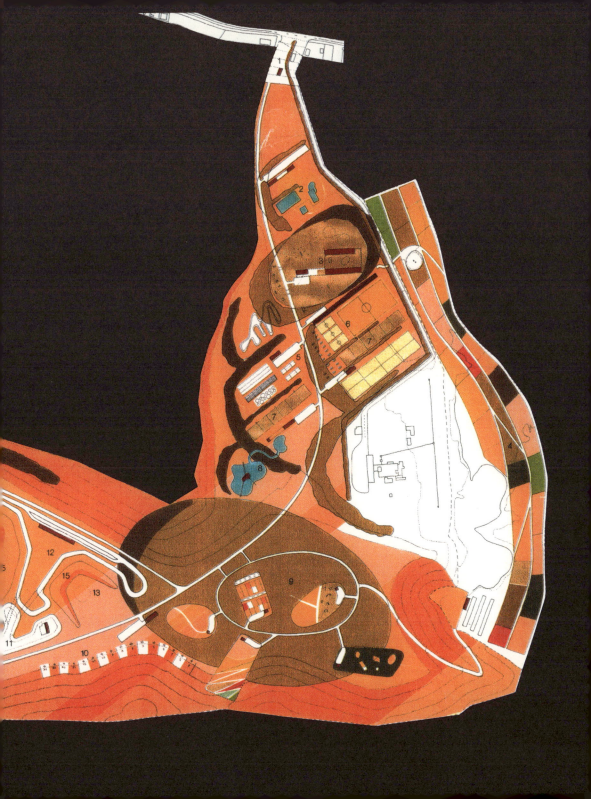

NEW RECYCLING PLAN FOR URB

The project is part of a group of projects that were to create a rational system for the
treatment and recycling of the waste, as well as the transformation and the incorporation of
its land into the future Southeast Regional Park, which was one of the city's most attractive
projects that were intended to even-out the social and environmental differences that
existed between the north and the south
The recycling plant concentrates a heterogeneous group of buildings for the selection and
processing of the refuse, storage, workshops and offices, all brought together beneath a
large, inclined green roof that echoes, as much, the gravitational character of the process
as it does the original hillside upon which it sits, "restored", taking advantage of the
compost that is produced. The building is wrapped with recycled polycarbonate that unifies
the various programmes and incorporates a museum area that has a route for visitors,
aimed at making the public more environmentally aware.

WASTE

The green roof, the polycarbonate, the light riveted structure and the interior finishes show this spirit, as they demonstrate the best environmental compromise that is currently possible with available techniques.

This building is composed of two complementary constructions: one is dedicated to the production of compost from organic waste, and the second is dedicated to the control and the weighing of the lorries that enter the enclosure. Both have been treated as though they were industrial objects that set up a dialogue with the scale and the singularity of the landscape, built using systems that are analogous to those used in the first building.

The centre has a life-span of twenty-five years, after which it will be recycled as a service building for the park or dismantled so that its components might be, themselves, recycled.

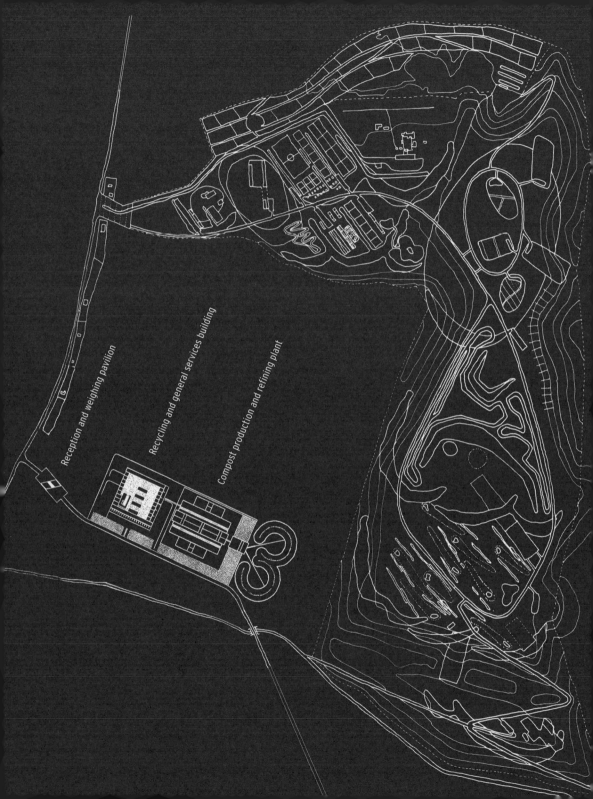

Reception and weighing pavilion

Recycling and general services building

Compost production and refining plant

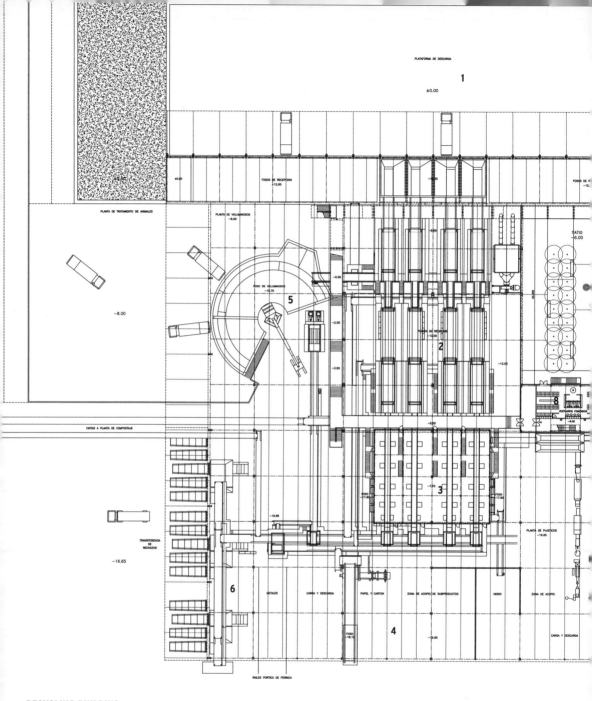

RECYCLING BUILDING

Overall plan: 1 Waste unloading area. 2 Mechanical waste separation. 3 Final selection. 4 Storage area for recycled material. 5 Area for bulky waste. 6 Transfer area to landfill (non-recyclable waste). 7 Reception and environmental room. 8 Locker rooms for personnel. 9 Parking for heavy vehicles. 10. Offices. 11 Cafeteria. 12 Museum and access to visitor center. 13 Roof access.

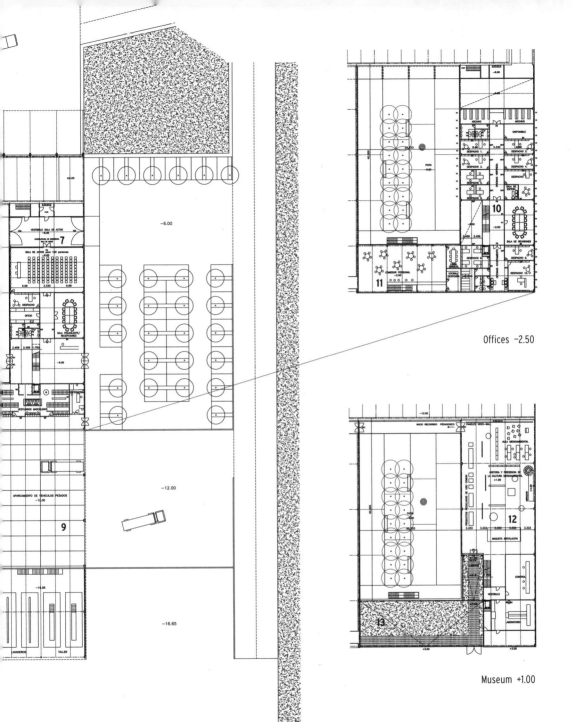

Offices −2.50

Museum +1.00

EDUARDO ARROYO

Everything flows and nothing remains... it seems.

We already know that living individuals tend to retain their own identity independently of the fluctuations of their environment. This is not so, however, for inanimate objects that succumb to the constant changes of their surroundings. It seems to be accepted, in the world of biology, that when the territory of a species is endangered, through environmental deterioration or the scarcity of food, nature imposes restrictions upon the reproductive urge. The males do not mate with the females who, in turn, become sterile. It is a familiar scenario.

Is it possible that because of our awareness of the latent danger of extinction that suddenly people feel an urge to preserve the dignity of objects and not to allow them to go beyond a corrupt old age, where they lose their function, that is so inevitably familiar to us.

And what if this millennial desire to exist again and for an everlasting return without fleeting endings, leads us to bring back to life, fictitiously, those things that surround us and that we accept as lives that have come to an end, to which the hope of survival is a distant cosmic brilliance?

And now we are moved to find out that the basin in which Auntie Polly washes her feet can, one day, become a Swedish toothbrush which might itself be transformed, in the not too distant future, into part of a polycarbonate wall, lit by the light of the Western sun on the Madridian steppes. Things tend to return to earth, to disappear. Only our frightened minds are capable of transforming their apparent squalor into some kind of strange beauty and to prevent them from reverting to their original state. Artifice, pure and simple.

But for a universal artifice, the consumerism that has forced us to reinvent our refuse, as well as the mechanisms of transformation and those spaces that are associated with them serve as an example. Like the great cathedrals of our time, comparable only with football

stadiums but somehow more anonymous, recycling plants are the new centres of the spiritual purification of stained objects. It is a process that is similar to the emotional and cathartic recycling of *Match on Sunday*. The world cleanses itself with rubbish dumps. Our consciences do so with sport-euphoric cheers.

Until very recently, the uncontrolled euphoria of commercialism has been to use-and-dump. As a consequence of this, dump-and-store has become the planet's nightmare. With the ecologist alarm-bell sounding at full volume, we have tried to substitute these binomial relationships for others called *use-and-reuse* or *dump-and-transform*, thus returning the dream of a smiling civilization to the populace.

And those smiles of a city that is thrilled to see how the surrounding landscape, that was becoming a duplicate of the Cantabrian mountain range that is made of rubbish bags, becomes tinged with green, with clean soil and ultra-sophisticated hydroponics plantations. Settled in this new landscape, there was a need for a building whose guts would be able to focus our gaze upon the depths of dirtiness —upon what is apparently despised. Within it resides our ability to look towards the future, like a telescope that witnesses the expansion of the universe. It is, without doubt, the symbol of the motivation and the will to see it through to the end. In a way, it is the mirror of the planning and the emotional control of a city, bestowing its own personality upon it: advanced, clean. From the point of view of the built object, it is a conscious effort to imagine what has never before existed as an architectural element, and so it does not have a form that we hold in our memory.

In the Valdemingómez Recycling Plant, there is a clear intention to integrate it into the landscape. There is an intention to open the process to the gaze of another and, perhaps, the poetic intention to use clean light. But perhaps the true 'idea of the rubbish dump' is in the linking of the buildings with the landscape depending on the mechanisms involved in the process of recycling: gravitational and mechanical in the case of those housed in the main building, or linear and chemical in the case of the composting building. It is a light architecture that is placed lightly upon the site, like dirt upon a surface: weightless from one viewpoint or camouflaged from another.

On this visit we come across two distinguished passers-by. Parmenides, on the exterior with his immanent gaze upon the world, intends to remain through the materialization of a group of buildings that are frozen on the landscape. They are silent and immutable, attempting to disappear under the carpet of vegetation. However, inside we greet Heraclitus. Everything is in a state of motion, change and uncertainty, a transcendental view of the transformation of matter and an uncomfortable programme with an industrial and systematic character with which certain architectures might fall into conflict. However I believe that herein lies the project's greatest success: the aggressive and unhealthy condition of the programme is softened by a bridge that leads into the surrounding landscape, rather like an improvised latrine in the middle of the jungle that is shielded from the sight of other simians by a silken skirt that was stolen from our travelling companion, which we almost feel pleasure to enter.

Valdemingómez is a spatial and personal journey. A group of sequential buildings and their obedient accompanying of the successive phases of the transformation of the residues. A landscape of different programmes that have an unlimited capacity for growth and an individualized response to each one of them. It is, therefore, a visual passage of apprenticeship, a sort of pathetic Tao, close to the waste of the city that forces us to live hand in hand with the journey that takes place inside. The delicate wrapping of this drama of perceptions, the raised walkways and the sequence of platforms instantly seduce us with their Piranesian vision of hoppers, grinders, conveyor belts and other mechanisms: *terminator-style*, where our imagination is aroused with perfect murders that are feverishly planned against our most beloved villains. A world that awakens those leisurely senses, our innocent cinematographic gaze.

But our innocence cannot hide from us the fact that the patient in this hospital is just refuse, dirtiness and left-over scraps that, prior to visiting the hoppers of surgery, display cosmetic face-lifts that are perfect for their imminent use. A close reference to the origin of the word, "cosmos" is a will to outline a new universe with a different order, a yearning to find those forms that represent the shamanic rituals that hold these architectures in their depths. From the washbasin into polycarbonate, from lettuce into methane, from Coca-Cola into aluminium sections. Buildings that feed themselves and are formed with their own produce, which happens to be nothing but *kk* –but at least it is *de luxe*[1].

Intelligent.

Manhattan Transfer (The Form of the Spectacle)

"Our nature resides in movement." Pascal

Truman Capote gave us one of the most exciting images of this closing century. It has been amplified to such an extent that it has been absorbed by the collective imagination until its strength has become almost undetectable. It is the story of that moment of any morning when the lives of New Yorkers criss-cross intensely through Central Station. For one moment the people lost their sense of "I" and became equal through their movement across the majestic vestibule with one collective consciousness of "going", but with the disturbing sensation that on arriving at their destination, they would never be the same again. They sensed that Central Station, like a giant machine, was steering and classifying them: some to the luxurious platform of the Boston Express, others to the overcrowded suburban trains and the rest to the dark depths of the metropolis.

In these times, our mass society is characterised by a horror of tranquillity, by the duality between the motive voyage of western invention and the stationary personal voyage imported from the Orient. In the Valdemingómez plant our dark passers-by, eternally returning,

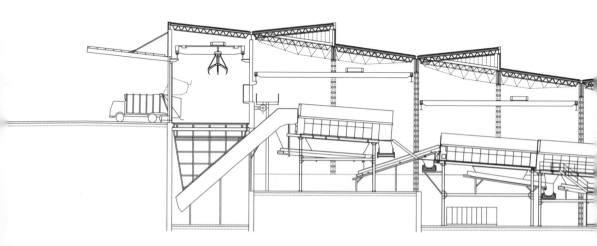

are thus the fleeting dregs of a society that is based on refuse, who will find their path, selecting it gravitationally in this large well-lit hall, always meeting with others of the same class on clearly differentiated levels. On their way to a new life, the materials accelerate or slow down, unaware of the great difference in scale between themselves and the building that shelters them, acquiring a velocity that is proportional to the affection that the society outside professes to have for them. Metals travel towards safety at high speeds on small express platforms at the highest level of the vestibule, like diamonds on a black Jewish kerchief. Cardboard, dirty and unpredictable, is directed towards large slow

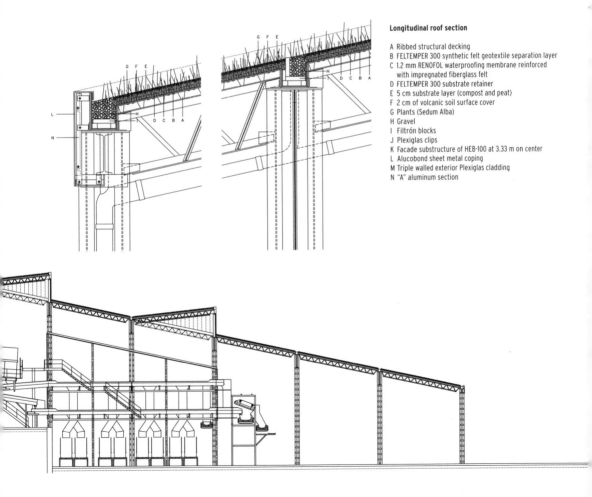

Longitudinal roof section

A Ribbed structural decking
B FELTEMPER 300 synthetic felt geotextile separation layer
C 1.2 mm RENOFOL waterproofing membrane reinforced
   with impregnated fiberglass felt
D FELTEMPER 300 substrate retainer
E 5 cm substrate layer (compost and peat)
F 2 cm of volcanic soil surface cover
G Plants (Sedum Alba)
H Gravel
I Filtrón blocks
J Plexiglas clips
K Facade substructure of HEB-100 at 3.33 m on center
L Alucobond sheet metal coping
M Triple walled exterior Plexiglas cladding
N "A" aluminum section

conveyor-belts, banished to the lowest levels and reminding us of the *homeless paradise* in any of our cities and that remains, perpetually, in our dark consciences.

The opening of this fascinating process to our gaze hinders our view of the building that houses it, and which is more silent but, somehow, more spectacular. A close look will reveal those careful openings for zenithal or lateral lighting, with their various degrees of polycarbonated translucence, depending of the needs of the system. Close to this jostling of material and light hybridizations, we will discover a precious patio, almost monastic in rendering, that seems to anticipate the possibility that the workers might make use of a place where they can pray that this indescribable machinery does not explode in their faces.

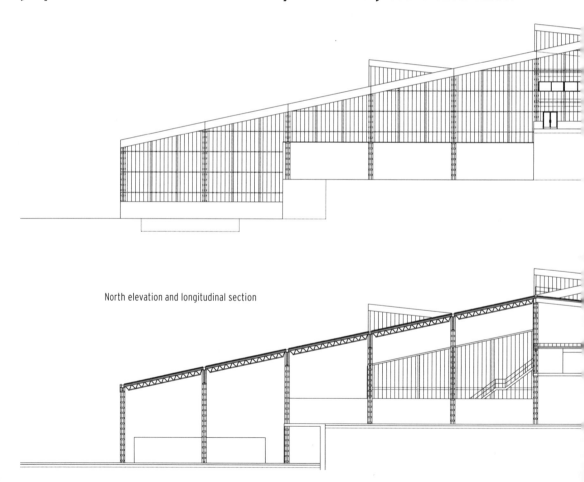

North elevation and longitudinal section

But the true refuse of this mechanistic, stratified society and the only redoubt of fertile life in this scenographic interchange is the organic refuse that is expelled from it into another, much less public, building that is, somehow, more mournful. It is a place for enclosing those pitiful products so that they rot in cells, closed to the outside, and are transformed into compost. It is something useful for this new recycling society that comes about through this other, Oriental-style transformation that is truly motionless in character.

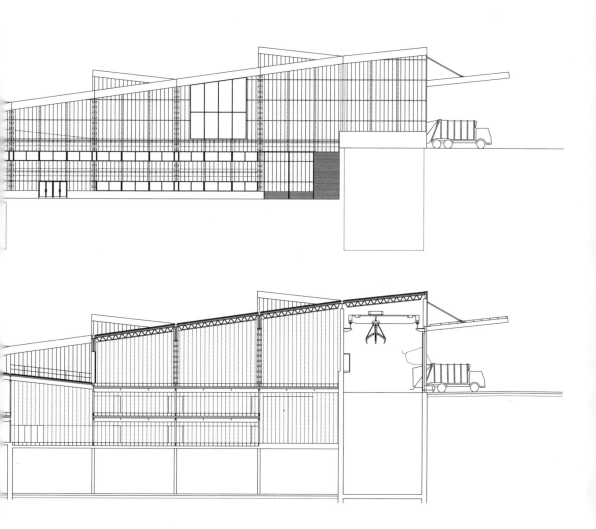

Sing Sing (The Form of Confinement)

"Mirror Mirror on the wall, Who is the fairest of us all?..."

Snow White's wicked stepmother

Almost all human beings live in the constant terror of the despair that is caused by their own existence and a fear of a scenario of physical decay. In the face of change, protean evolution, it seems that the only possibility that remains for man is that of him ordering, moulding and enclosing the world in a stable appearance of immutability and harmony.

A prisoner of its own squalor, the organic material that is expelled from the main building is ordered in an enclosure of large concrete vats, whose doors only open, simultaneously, to give their contents a tremendous jolt. The architecture of this composting building becomes a scale-less powerful machine and its design disappears as it is reduced to a mere structural support for the cladding and of those complex non-architectural mechanisms.

Faced with the apparent three-dimensional chaos of the selection mechanism which made necessary a single volume building with a perimetrical character, the compost is treated in a linear, bi-dimensional way, within an architectural structure that is Alcatraz-like and similar to an armoured bank safe, where an atmosphere of mystery cloaks the invisibility of the decomposition process. With temperatures inside the upper vats reaching more than one hundred degrees, the interest that is aroused in our senses, has more to do with the sensuality of what is invisible but intuited, rather than with the immediacy of the image in real time.

COMPOST PRODUCTION AND REFINING PLANT

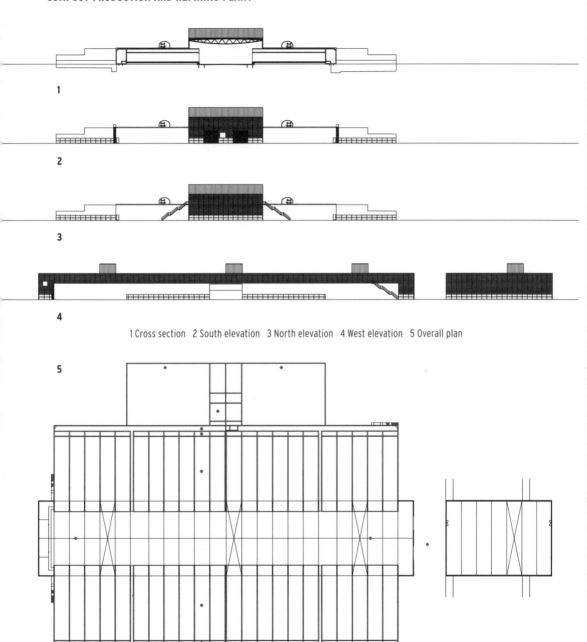

1

2

3

4

1 Cross section   2 South elevation   3 North elevation   4 West elevation   5 Overall plan

5

Rockefeller (The Form of Mistrust)

"The virtue is in producing, without possessing nor dominating..." Tao Te King

This millennium that is coming to an end seems to do so in honour of the ecological thinking that has, once again, shown us the meaning of our limitations and has made clear Mother Earth's rebellion against our ambitious projects of unlimited growth and business deals.

Submerged beneath all of this architectural effort lies the sign of our times: a strong business that is rigorously protected by those who control it. Thus, all lorries are weighed and classified on entering or leaving in a small building that comes straight out of a fantastic ABC book (The building is in the shape of a letter "T") [2] and in which one could expect to hear the bell of an old clocking-in machine sound, or perhaps, more authentically, some other bureaucrat yell "tip!" for each lorry that checks in.

This check-in point is an oyster with cold and sophisticated materials on the outside: polycarbonates and steel protect it from its surroundings. An atypical warmth takes over the interior and is embodied in one material that has itself been recycled from wood chips in the form of three-ply panels. They are as seductive as mother-of-pearl, sheltering the Madrid Council's economic pearl. One feels an agreeable sensation because the use of such a humble material hardly reflects the figures that the computers in this built caprice deal with.

Crossing this small entrance is the beginning of an initiation rite, after which we will no longer see the capricious surrounding landscape in the same traditional way that we did ten minutes before, on entering. All that we had before perceived as natural will change into pure artifice during our visit. On concluding the visit, when we return to our normal state of consciousness, the only thing that we will perceive as belonging to this fictitious landscape will be Iñaki's and Juan's cosmic buildings as though they had been there forever to produce this landscape of madness.

EDUARDO ARROYO

1 *Kk de Luxe* was the name of one of the first pop bands of the *movida madrileña* -or Madridian Scene, which was a cultural movement which sprang up in Madrid in the 1980's.
2 The original Spanish text uses a play on words, with which the author liken the T-shape of the building to the letter "T" with which the word "tacaño" begins and which translates into English as "mean". (Translator note)

RECEPTION AND WEIGHING PAVILION

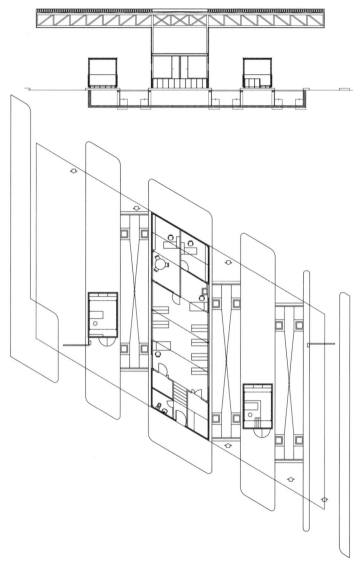

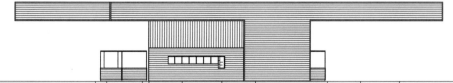

VALDEMINGOMEZ 1999

LUIS ASIN

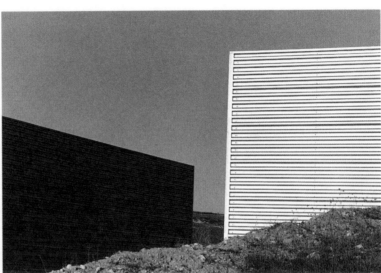

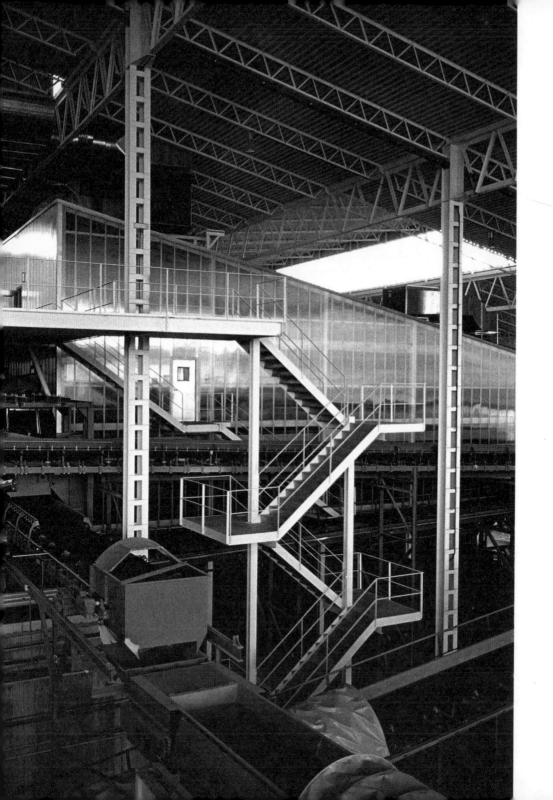

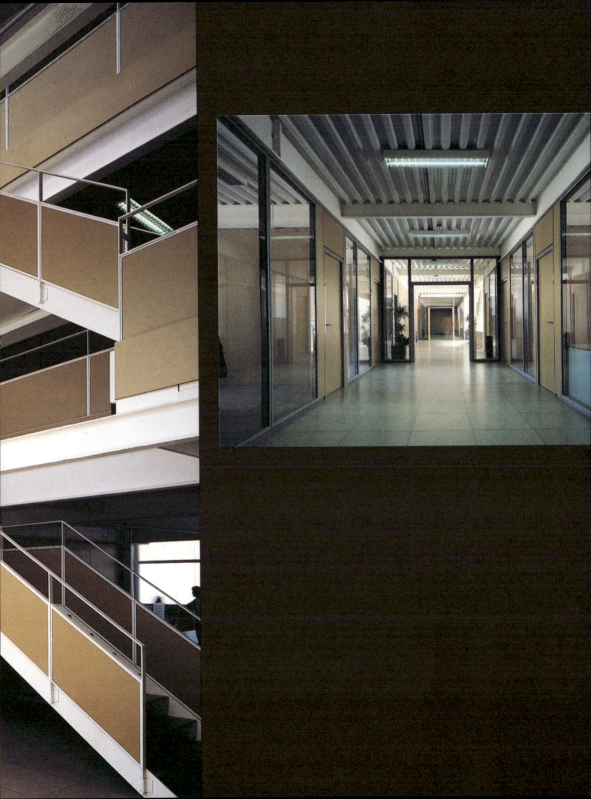

SOME CLUES

ANA YAGÜES

With the project of the Valdemingómez Rubbish Dump, the architects explain architecture's ability to transform the hidden into the visible and the industrial into the public. They call this redefinition of reality through modifications of the convention that transforms something that is neutral or even vulgar into something that is unusual and seductive, "pragmatic imagination". Each of the three buildings that they have built there proves that this is not just a theoretical goal but something tangible: something that has always been known as "an experience". But when they explain Valdemingómez, and on the various site visits that I have shared with them −some of them at times and under circumstances that are frankly indescribable− my attention shifts from the buildings to the relationships between objects, to what in the fifties used to be called "space" and is now refered to by some as a "landscape of events".

I see the open mouths of the schoolchildren who, astonished, watch how orange peel and tin cans pass by on conveyor belts like groups of Japanese tourists at the airport. They look tiny up there and they remind me of myself, when I visited the Coca-Cola factory and its secret formula, with the same eyes and the same open mouth. When the visitors are teenagers, their faces take on a hint of disbelief and eroticism with the attraction of filth. It is the same expression of the main character in *The Graduate*. I can imagine the same expressions on the faces of the medical students who attend, from a viewing balcony, a dissection for the first time, and I admire the subtlety of an almost invisible architecture that makes such marvels of our most foul excrements. Life in its most obscene and filthy form is down there. It is there thanks to the aseptic calmness of the enclosure that contains it: a hygenic medieval theatre that redoubles the beauty of what is most ugly, transforming it into the star of a performance of *Dirty Realism*, which even outshines Raymond Carver's best story.

The same thing occurs outside, from the moment that we enter the plant or even before on the rural access road that is colonized today by a tirelessly working-class, marginalized community: one's attention is diverted away from the objects and their relationships to each other and towards the landscape that has been produced. Horses, dogs, lorries and trucks loaded with unlikely objects move between the mountains of refuse that flower in spring like the most delicate garden: a spectacle whose magnificence embraces its squalor. The monumental T that Iñaki and Juan have placed at the entrance disappears as one watches it: what we see is the radical division of the space that it produces. To its left, the plant's main building emerges from the ground and invites us to discover it. To its right is a naked and infinite expanse upon which the lorries, like mechanical ants, build a new hill with refuse. With this radical gesture we immediately understand the spatial relationships and processes, the unloading in the pits, the institutional facade, the routes and the hierarchy between the pieces. The same thing occurs in the recycling plant, in which all of the views are oblique and are directed towards the landscape, the other constructions, the machines or the emptiness. This building rises towards the planted roof and then, after gazing at Madrid with its great Cyclopean eye, it sinks until it fuses with the land: another artificial hill that is built upon this landscape where all natural accidents are the products of man's work. And the compost down there, silent, accepting its humble role as manager of the new, constantly mutating landscape.

If we were still uncertain about exactly what the areas of impunity were, we now know: the hidden city revealed, mirror games between respectable architecture and the hybridization of marginalization and nature: a cocktail whose revitalizing effects are well known by Iñaki and Juan. The exhibition that the Col·legi d'Arquitectes de Catalunya has dedicated to them —a timely tribute with a refreshing political perspective— materializes this mirror game with its content and its montage. Various projects create a landscape which we do not know whether to classify in the categories of the urban or the natural, the cultured or the popular, the commercial or the alternative. This is the amalgam with which they nourish their projects, not only for their formalization, but also to build, through them, a particular vision of the world. I can imagine the pleasure that they felt when they took on a project such as Valdemingómez in which both the programme and the materials coincide with their interest in exploring creative techniques and processes that are based upon the use and the decontextualization of existing materials.

It is, perhaps, in their most monumental project: the Algeciras tower, where their technique of recycling design and their cosmic ambition can best be seen. Somehow their other projects are integrated into this artefact that relates to the landscape, that makes city in as far as it sets up a dialogue with the landscape. The precious excercise that is known as Colmenarejo is contained in its facade, with the wicker transformed into cork as an acknowlegment to the woods that surrounds the city. We see the echo of the Gordillo House in its apartments, the offices for RENFE and the Ministry of the Interior are contained in its alternating voids and we recognise Simancas and the El Retiro Pavilion in its gymnasiums. In its raised gardens and in its dual composition we see the Plaza de Castilla and the Zaragoza projects repeated: raised in one case and flattened in the other.

Their inclination towards tall buildings: the skyscraper, as a symbolic expression of modernity was already well known. However, it was difficult to understand their interest in the transformations that this type of building had been undergoing throughout the twentieth century until it became an object of a different nature: hybrid and complex. Now we can see to what extent that interest corresponded with their way of understanding architecture. It was more to do with explaining their method than with the description of a building type. In the Algeciras project, Ábalos and Herreros revisit, not only their best projects, but also the modern skyscraper, transforming both experiences into a new and surprising object that is more concerned with geography than with history. Through the recycling of inherited modernity and by mixing it with a new sensibility towards contemporary culture and landscape, a new city that contains modernity but that is, at the same time, decidedly different is glimpsed. To recycle is to introduce into the circle of life something that had been used up by transforming it through physical or chemical processes capable of bestowing it with new properties or uses. Terence Riley, the architecture curator of the MoMA in New York, understood their architecture in this way when he said, "If younger architects, such as Iñaki Ábalos and Juan Herreros, have found Mies' legacy to be so fertile today, it may be because they no longer need the master's or his disciples' permission to use it. They are no more 'Miesian' than Andrea Palladio was 'Albertian': they have simply absorbed this century's great architectural lessons without letting the architect absorb them." The Algeciras or Valdemingómez projects are two eloquent examples that show glimmerings of what is still to come. Curiously, it is a significant coincidence that Algeciras means "green island" and that Ábalos and Herreros have imagined Madrid as a green island. It is from the periphery, from the South of the South that Algeciras is to Europe, just as Valdemingómez is the South of Madrid, that their personal trajectory is being built, transfering what is learned onto the limits of the urban towards the centre of the city.

I conclude. The recent work of Ábalos and Herreros is not just a virtuosic excercise of surfaces and building techniques. It consists, rather, of the establishing of mixtures, connections and spatial relationships, in shaping coreographies that make all of the pieces work in a unified and compact way: the existing and the new, people and objects, the city and the landscape, the materials and the space. Their architecture embraces the legacy of modernity in order to turn it around and to produce images with it that would seem to be new and radical to the unattentive observer, but that hoard all of the experiences of the twentieth century. This tool is used with great intensity to amplify the idea of what is public, developing a careful attitude towards those programmes and places which architecture has, until now, avoided. The result is a work that is surprisingly unified and coherent, a professional biography that is built around the margins of conventional trajectories and commissions, and will, surely, soon surprise us again with another of their iconoclastic pirouettes that will force us to rethink what, until now, we thought we knew. ANA YAGÜES

Iñaki Ábalos (San Sebastián, 1956) and **Juan Herreros** (San Lorenzo de El Escorial, 1958) have worked together since 1984. Since 1992 they have directed and coordinated the International Multimedia League, which is an organization dedicated to contributing to the simplification and intensification of artistic practice. Since 1994, they have edited *ExitLMI, Documentos de Arquitectura*. **Ángel Jaramillo** (Almería, 1968) became an associate architect in the practice in 1997.

Publications
1987   *Le Corbusier. Rascacielos*, Ayuntamiento de Madrid
1991   *Iñaki Ábalos y Juan Herreros. Seis Proyectos (1987-1990)*, Madrid, COAM
1992   *Técnica y Arquitectura en la Ciudad Contemporánea*, Madrid, Nerea
         (English edition: The MIT Press, 2000)
1993   *Ábalos & Herreros*, Barcelona, Gustavo Gili
1997   *Áreas de Impunidad / Areas of Impunity*, Barcelona, Actar
1999   *Natural-Artificial*, ExitLMI, Madrid
2000   *Ábalos & Herreros: Reciclando Madrid / Recycling Madrid*, Barcelona, Actar

Teaching Activities
1984-1988   Construction tutors, ETSA Madrid
1988-   Design tutors, ETSA Madrid
1996-1997   Buell Book Fellows and Visiting Teachers, Columbia University, New York
1997-1999   Diploma Unit Masters, Architectural Association, London
1998-1999   Professeurs invités, École Polytechnique Federale, Lausanne
                  Various courses, seminars and workshops in Spain, the European Union, the United States
                  and Latin America.

Solo Exhibitions

1991   *Seis Proyectos*. Colegio Oficial de Arquitectos de Madrid (travelling)
1996   *Áreas de Impunidad*. Facultad de Arquitectura de Montevideo
1997   *Concursos*. Museo de Arte Moderno, Bogotá
2000   *Ábalos & Herreros: reciclando / recycling Madrid*, Colegio Oficial de Arquitectos de Cataluña, Barcelona (travelling)

Collective Exhibitions

1993   *Architektur*. Gallerie Max Hetzler and Gallerie Philomena Magers, Köln
1994   *Enseña tus heridas*. Entorno Experimental de Actividades Artísticas, Madrid
1995   *Light Construction*. MoMA, New York (curator: Terence Riley) (travelling)
1996   *Present and Futures*. UIA / Centro de Cultura Contemporánea, Barcelona
       (curator: Ignasi de Solà-Morales)
       Less is More. UIA / Colegio Oficial de Arquitectos de Cataluña, Barcelona
       (curators: Josep Maria Montaner and E. Savi) (travelling)
1997   *New territories, New landscapes*, MACBA, Barcelona (curator: Eduard Bru)
1998   *Fabricaciones / Fabrications*. MACBA, MoMA, Wexner, SFMoMA
       (curators: Xavier Costa, Terence Riley, Mark Robbins and Aaron Betsky)
1999   *Arquitectura para cultura*. The IVth Sâo Paulo International Architecture Biennial
2000   *Pabellón de España* and *E-City*, The 7th International Architecture Exhibition. Venice
2000   *Metápolis 2.0*. Barcelona
2000   Spanish Pavilion. Expo Hannover

Built Works

1986-1987   Three Water-treatment Plants. Villalba, Guadarrama, Majadahonda
1988-1990   Two Sports Halls. Simancas, Valladolid
1988-1995   52 Housing Units on the M-30, Madrid
1989   Office Building for RENFE, Fuencarral, Madrid

1990-1991	Office Building for the Ministerio del Interior, Madrid
1991-1998	Parque de Europa (455 housing units), Palencia (design stages only)
1992-1995	Town Hall and Cultural Centre, Cobeña, Madrid
1994-1996	Gordillo House, Villanueva de la Cañada, Madrid
1995-2003	Library in Usera, Madrid
1996-1999	Recycling Plant for Urban Waste, Madrid
1997-2004	Urban Planning of the Ramos Area, Río de Janeiro
1997-1999	Village Hall and Square, Colmenarejo, Madrid
1998-2002	Office Building for the Junta de Andalucía, Almería
1998-2000	Gordillo Workshop, Villanueva de la Cañada, Madrid
1998-2000	Environmental Classroom, Arico, Tenerife
1999-2001	Varsawsky House, Formentor, Mallorca
1999-2001	Central Administration Building, Universidad de Extremadura, Mérida
2000-2001	Gymnasics Pavilion, Madrid

Projects

1986	Planning of the Plaza de Castilla. Madrid
1989	Planning of Diagonal. Barcelona
1991	Dune Park in Doñana. Huelva
1993	Channelling of River Guadalhorce. Málaga
1994	Industrialized Housing Units AH
1997	Architekturforum. Bonn
1999	AVE Train Station and Interchange Terminal. Zaragoza
1999	El Mirador: Mixed-use tower block In The Bay of Algeciras. Cádiz
2000	Landscape Recuperation and the Valdemingómez Rubbish Dump Educational Centre. Madrid

Awards

1987   Second prize: Planning of the Plaza de Castilla, Ayuntamiento de Madrid

1988   First prize: 52 housing units on the M-30, EMV, Madrid
The Madrid Council Award for Architecture and Urban Design for the exhibition
Le Corbusier. Rascacielos
Second Prize: Opera: square, housing units and interchange terminal, COAM, Madrid

1989   First prize: Office building for RENFE
Runner-up: Housing & City. Planning of Diagonal, Barcelona, COAC
First prize: Parque de Europa, Diputación de Palencia

1991   The Madrid Council Award for Architecture and Urban Design. (Office building for RENFE)
COAM Architecture Prize. (Office building for RENFE)

1993   First prize: Urban planning of Abando Ibarra. Ayuntamiento de Bilbao and COAVN, Bilbao
Sellected. II Bienal de Arquitectura Española. MOPTMA. (Simancas Sports Hall)

1995   First prize: Usera Public Library, Comunidad de Madrid
Selected. III Bienal de Arquitectura Española. MOPTMA.
(Office building for the Ministerio del Interior)

1997   First prize: Recycling Plant for Urban Waste, Ayuntamiento de Madrid
First prize: Río Cidade 2 Project. Área Ramos, Ayuntamiento de Río de Janeiro
First prize: Headquarters for the Junta de Andalucía, Almería, Junta de Andalucía
COAM Architecture Prize. (Gordillo House)
Comunidad de Madrid Prize. (Gordillo House)
Comunidad de Madrid Prize. (52 housing units on the M-30)
Iberfad de Arquitectura Finalist. (Gordillo House)

1999   Ajuntament de Barcelona Prize. (*Fabrications* Installation)
First prize: General Service Building for the Universidad de Extremadura,
Consejería de Educación y Juventud, Junta de Extremadura, Mérida
Second prize: Urban planning of the El Mirador area, Ayuntamiento de Algeciras

2000   Ayuntamiento de Madrid Architecture Prize. Recycling plant for urban waste, Valdemingómez.
Madrid

WORKS AND PROJECTS

VILLAGE HALL AND SQUARE COLMENAREJO, MADRID 1997-1999

Clients **Comunidad de Madrid and Ayuntamiento de Colmenarejo**
Architects **Iñaki Ábalos, Juan Herreros and Ángel Jaramillo**
Collaborators **David Franco and Carolina González Vives**
Structural Engineers **Juan Gómez**
Quantity Surveyor and Services **Juan José Núñez**
Site Architects **Ábalos & Herreros, Ángel Valdivieso**
Technical Control **Laura Martín, Óscar Miranzo and José Antonio Rodríguez**

VILLA FG MADRID 1997-1999

Architects **Iñaki Ábalos, Juan Herreros and Ángel Jaramillo**
Collaborators **David Franco, Carmen Izquierdo, Pablo Martínez Capdevila and Renata Sentkiewicz**
Models **Escala 9, Andrea Buchner and Renata Sentkiewicz**
Structural Engineers **Obiol y Moya**
Computer Graphics **Gestalt**
Services **José María Cruz and Pedro José Blanco**
Facade **Cristina Iglesias and Patrick Blanck (vertical garden)**
Landscape Architects **Fernando Valero and Bet Figueras**
Lighting **Josep Maria Civit**
Quantity Surveyor **Juan José Núñez**
Furnishing **Artificio**
Interior Design **Félix Fernández**

EL MIRADOR: MIXED-USE TOWER IN THE BAY OF ALGECIRAS CÁDIZ 1999

National Ideas Competition (Second Prize)
Client **Ayuntamiento de Algeciras**
Architects **Iñaki Ábalos, Juan Herreros and Ángel Jaramillo**
Collaborators **Jakob Hense and Renata Sentkiewicz**
Model **Escala 9**

AVE TRAIN STATION AND INTERCHANGE TERMINAL ZARAGOZA 1999

Architecture and Engineering Competition
Client **GIF**
Architects **Iñaki Ábalos, Juan Herreros and Ángel Jaramillo**
Collaborators **Uriel Fogué, Jakob Hense and Renata Sentkiewicz**
Structural Engineering **Ove Arup**
Project Manager **José Luis Burgos, Lorenzo Jaro, Juan Alberto García de Cubas and Asunción Rodríguez Montejano (MECSA)**
Models **Escala 9**
Computer Graphics **AG & Asociados**

GREEN HOUSE POZUELO, MADRID 1997

Architects **Iñaki Ábalos, Juan Herreros and Ángel Jaramillo**
Collaborators **Mª Auxiliadora Gálvez, Carolina González Vives y Carmen Izquierdo**
Model **Aurelie Beriot and Andrea Buchner**
Structural Engineers **Juan Gómez**
Computer Graphics **Gestalt**
Quantity Surveyor **Miguel Ángel Rica**

GYMNASTICS PAVILION IN EL RETIRO MADRID 1999

Client **Instituto Municipal de Deportes del Ayuntamiento de Madrid**
Architects **Iñaki Ábalos, Juan Herreros and Ángel Jaramillo**
Collaborators **Renata Sentkiewicz and Fermina Garrido**
Model and Computer Graphics **Jakob Hense**

VALDEMINGÓMEZ DUMP. THE LANDSCAPE TRANSFORMATION OF MADRID'S OLD RUBBISH DUMP [1997]

Client **Vertresa-RWE Process**
Architects **Iñaki Ábalos, Juan Herreros and Ángel Jaramillo**
Collaborators **Aurelie Beriot, Ángel Borrego, Cristina Díaz Moreno, David Franco, Efrén García-Grinda, Rafael Hernández and Pablo Martínez Capdevila**
Landscape Architect **Fernando Valero**
Models **Escala 9**
Multimedia **Lunatus**

NEW RECYCLING PLANT FOR URBAN WASTE
MADRID 1996-1999

Competition for Firms
Client **Vertresa-RWE Process and Ayuntamiento de Madrid**
Architects **Iñaki Ábalos, Juan Herreros and Ángel Jaramillo**
Collaborators **Aurelie Beriot, Ángel Borrego, Cristina Díaz Moreno, David Franco, Mª Auxiliadora Gálvez, Efrén García-Grinda and Pablo Martínez Capdevila**
Models **Escala 9, David Franco and Pablo Martínez Capdevila**
Structural Engineers **Obiol y Moya**
Engineering **Servicios Técnicos de Vertresa. Team leader: Fernando Valledor**
Services **José María Cruz and Pedro José Blanco**
Landscape Architect **Fernando Valero**
Environmental Impact Studies **Javier Ceballos**
Geological Report **Andrés Carbó**
Multimedia **Lunatus**
Computer Graphics **Gestalt**
Project Manager **Juan Sempere (IMES)**
Technical Control **Juan Espinosa (Vertresa)**
Quantity Surveyors **Miguel Ángel Rica and José Torras**

AUTHORS

Ignasi de Solà-Morales is an architect, critic, historian and professor in Barcelona, where he was one of the architects responsible for the reconstruction of the Barcelona Pavilion. He is the author of *Diferencias. Topografía de la arquitectura contemporánea* as well as various texts on the history and theory of architecture that have been published both in Europe and the United States.

Pep Xurret is an opinion collective made up of architects from Barcelona who were born at the end of the sixties, including Iñaki Baquero, Josep Bohigas and Francesc Pla (BOPBAA).

Eduardo Arroyo graduated in architecture at the ETSAM in 1988, and has taught design at the same school since 1996. He founded NO.MAD in 1990. His projects and buildings have received various prizes and have been widely published. He is the author of the book *Al otro lado del espejo*.

Luis Asín began studying Law at the Universidad Complutense de Madrid, leaving the course in its fourth year. He moved to California to study Photography in various universities and finally graduated from the San Francisco Art Institute in 1992. He has exhibited his work in both individual and group exhibitions. His work has recently been published in a book titled *Luis Asín* (published by Caja Madrid in 1999).

Ana Yagües graduated in Art and Philosophy. She is also a writer and a musical critic. She has published *Los placeres de lo obsceno* and *Tecnopop*.